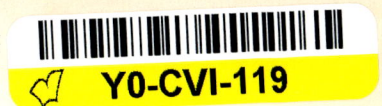

THE WORLD CRISIS
AND ITS MEANING

BOOKS BY FELIX ADLER

The World Crisis and Its Meaning

Marriage and Divorce

Life and Destiny

The Religion of Duty

The Moral Instruction of Children

THE WORLD CRISIS
AND ITS MEANING

BY

FELIX ADLER

NEW YORK AND LONDON
D. APPLETON AND COMPANY
1915

Copyright, 1915,
By D. APPLETON AND COMPANY

Printed in the United States of America

PREFACE

The matter of these chapters was originally couched in the language of public addresses and, with slight revision, the form and arrangement have been left undisturbed.

The author desires to express acknowledgment to Mr. George E. O'Dell, who has kindly read the proof sheets.

CONTENTS

CHAPTER		PAGE
I.	THE WORLD CRISIS AND ITS MEANING	1
II.	MILITARISM AND ITS EULOGISTS	30
III.	AMERICAN IDEALS CONTRASTED WITH GERMAN AND ENGLISH	58
IV.	THE ILLUSION AND THE IDEAL OF INTERNATIONAL PEACE	81
V.	CIVILIZATION AND PROGRESS IN THE LIGHT OF THE PRESENT WAR	111
VI.	THE MORAL AWAKENING OF THE WEALTHY	145
VII.	AN ETHICAL PROGRAM OF SOCIAL REFORM	172
VIII.	ETHICAL DEVELOPMENT EXTENDING THROUGHOUT LIFE	207

THE WORLD CRISIS AND ITS MEANING

I

THE WORLD CRISIS AND ITS MEANING

THE feeling that should predominate in America at this time is grief, not wrath. Since the world began there has been no such war. But the things now happening are too vast for spite and ancestral animosities, or even for the indulgence of moral indignation. What is it that has thrown civilization so suddenly out of its reckoning? Why this descent from the levels of culture and broadening brotherhood into the depths of brutality? Why do the peasants leave the harvests ungathered, to be themselves mowed down by a sharp, bloody scythe? Why are the gates of the universities closed? Why do the younger generation of scientists abandon their researches into the secrets of nature, prophetic of a beneficent extension of human knowledge, in order to join in the work of destruction? Why do the finest intelligences, the mental élite, fall in line with the dull, equally to lay down their heads on the great block? Why does the musician set aside his instrument on which he was wont to discourse music that touched and uplifted the soul, in order to mingle his voice with the hoarse cries of squadrons advancing to the charge, or with the despairing wail of the wounded? Why do fathers and husbands leave wives and children to slay other fathers and husbands who also have left clinging dear ones across the fatal border? Why do youths reared in all the gentleness of highbred social intercourse, suddenly take, as if they were beasts of the jungle, to the work of slaughter? The voice of lamentation is heard from Ramah; it is Rachel weeping for her children. It is the mother of humanity weeping for all those dead of many nations.

A great cloud has settled on the world. We are at the center of the darkness. But it behoves us to move from the center and seek to discover a ray of light, a ray of hope. Everyone at this time feels the immense desire to do something; to witness this unspeakable calamity and not stir a finger seems intolerable. We can contribute to the funds of the Red Cross Society in order somewhat to diminish the suffering caused by the war, and every instinct of humanity will impel us to do this. But for every wound we staunch in this way there will be countless wounds received which we cannot reach to alleviate. What else, then, can we do?

The United States is the one great nation not embroiled in the present conflict. Its favorable opinion is eagerly sought. It possesses a large measure of actual and potential authority. When the time for settlement comes, its counsel will be called for and will carry great weight. What compact of concord shall America recommend to the nations of Europe now at war? What safeguards shall she propose to prevent the recurrence of like disasters? To prepare the nation so that its voice shall ring out clear and true is work to be done from now on. In order that we may be in a fit state to perform this high office of counselor, which neither superior merit nor our form of government has assigned us, but our fortunate continental position between sea and sea, we must clear our mental eyes, so that we may correctly discern the radical flaw in our civilization that has made possible this huge *débâcle*. We must achieve a true diagnosis before we can recommend a remedy; and we must also, in the interest of a true diagnosis, be willing to lay aside our pet theories and to question sharply all the familiar panaceas, such as disarmament, the Court at the Hague, an international police, the destruction of militarism in Germany, the dethronement of kings, or socialism. Panaceas are cure-alls and we must distrust them; we cannot cure, if we do cure, till we have recognized the nature of the disease.

Now this, according to the opinion of many, is militarism. It is widely believed that if militarism could be broken where it is most pronounced and efficient, disarmament, or a great reduction of armaments, might follow, and the tortured world be freed to live in peace.

But is militarism the malady? It concerns us to the last degree not to mistake a mere symptom for the disease itself. We need an exact definition of the word in order to know with what we are dealing. Militarism involves, first, the existence of a class of professional experts sufficiently numerous to possess its *esprit de corps;* secondly, the expenditure of a large fraction of the national income for the maintenance and perfecting of the army and the fleet; thirdly, the obligatory military service of all male citizens—a year, two years or three years being required of every man in the flower of his age for the purpose of training, and a longer period ensuing during which he is liable to be called on to serve in case of need; fourthly, the inevitable concentration of power in the hands of the ruler of the state, whether prime minister, president or emperor. These four traits are typical, and the decisive point on which we must fix our attention is that militarism so defined exists wherever the preparation for war has become a regular business.

Militarism is only a symptom. If we wish to put the blame rightly or, setting aside the question of blame, if we wish to place the proximate cause rightly, let us place it on the shoulders of science. It is science, which has been so great a benefactor of the human race in some directions, that has also conjured up the new perils which invade the earth, the sea, and the air. It is with the help of science that inventive intelligence has built the aeroplanes and the dirigibles that scatter bombs, the dreadful siege-guns that tore to pieces the steel-capped forts of Liège, the submarines and the wandering mines that sow the sea with death. It is the hand of science that is evident in the complex arrangements for the rapid mobilization of troops, the provisioning of armies, the supplying of ammunition, the hurling of millions of troops across frontiers and from one frontier to another. It is the science embodied in modern warfare that accounts for the monstrous overgrowth of militarism in continental Europe, the disproportionate extent to which it absorbs the energies and fastens itself upon the vitality of modern peoples. And the salient features of militarism also are thus explained; the vast sums expended on the means of war are accounted for by the complexity and the costliness of the weapons which science and inventive genius have created.

Again, the long period of time required to construct the modern battleship, the siege-gun and the like armaments explains why, in times of peace, the preparations are not interrupted. If the necessary means of self-defense could be extemporized, if the weapons were just swords or lances or bludgeons, the nation whose liberties were invaded might trust to the enthusiasm of the moment to supply the means for resisting aggression. But enthusiasm and self-sacrifice plus extemporized weapons are powerless in the face of cold-blooded violence armed with the irresistible instruments which science has created.

There is, of course, another side to the intrusions of science into the business of war which ought in fairness not to be left unnoticed. It has been said with evident truth, in view of these bombs thrown from the air, these machine-guns stretching whole battalions dead and wounded upon the ground within a few moments, that man when he uses his brain, unbridled by the moral inhibitions, is the most dangerous of animals. But I have had touch with professional members of the military class in various countries and I have not found them to be ogres. They are generally courteous gentlemen living on small salaries, studious and hard-working. They believe war to be a necessary evil. Some of them, indeed, go further, and regard it as the source of the chivalric virtues, which they believe would perish if the sanguinary trials of strength between nations should cease. In this they are certainly mistaken. But the very science involved in their occupation, the difficulty of the technical problems which they have to meet, the exercise of high intellectual faculties which is required of them, fascinates them, and tends to make them forget the horrid butchery which to us is the outstanding fact in war. It is in a similar way that you will sometimes find medical men and surgeons so engrossed in the science of their calling that they come to regard the patient only as a "case" and that the saving of life, the humane aspect of their profession, is almost forgotten.

It concerns us, then, to recognize clearly that the dominion of militarism is not due solely, or even principally, to the arrogant spirit and the undisciplined ambitions of those who swing this huge engine of militarism to do its work. *The machine-gun is the counterpart of the machine loom.* Just as the substitution of machinery for hand-tools under the patronage of science has made it possible for those who own the machine to oppress the laborer, so the creation of all this enginery of war has made it possible for the rulers—and not for them alone, but, as I shall presently urge, for the peoples who support and willingly follow their rulers —to throw back for centuries the civilization which has been so painfully built up. The human race has run into a sort of impasse both

THE WORLD CRISIS AND ITS MEANING

in industry and war. The fertile mind of man has produced in both cases new servants and ministers of men's passions. The machine obsesses and controls mankind.

How shall the power of militarism be broken? Only by a new attitude, an inner spiritual change; nothing less than that will answer. There is no short-cut to relief. The human race will surely have to struggle for a long time against the incubus that rests upon it, gradually lightening it, but not shaking it off by one decisive act. There are some who believe that the backbone of militarism can be broken in the present war, which, with all its horrors, will, they think, be worth while because it is to be the last great war that the peoples will wage. I wish I could console myself by sharing their belief, but such optimism does not seem to me to be warranted. Already Mr. Nansen in Norway and some writers in England are pleading for universal military service in countries that hitherto have been free from it. Should the Dual Alliance win, the iron yoke will be riveted more firmly than ever. Should the Allies win, there will be Russia to be reckoned with—Russia, with its vast resources as yet scarcely touched on the surface;

THE WORLD CRISIS AND ITS MEANING

with a population that has swelled from sixty-five millions in the middle of the last century to one hundred and forty millions at the present day—Russia with the hands of its autocracy strengthened, and its ambitions intensified by victory. We hear much about the general exhaustion that will follow the struggle. Is this likely to be more than temporary in the case of a country like Russia or Germany, however much she may for the time be crippled? Did not Prussia lie trampled and bleeding on the ground, crushed under the heel of the French conqueror—to rise with renewed vigor on the battlefields of Leipzig and Waterloo? And if Germany should be broken and dismembered, will not the thirst for revenge simply be transferred from one bank of the Rhine to the other?

No; I see no hope of peace, no promise of anything better than a temporary truce, to be followed by new struggles for the chastisement of the offenders. Perhaps for centuries to come the nails of war must still be driven through the hands and feet of humanity. But out of the crucifixion shall come transfiguration. It may be that even out of the throes of this present fearful conflict will be born among

THE WORLD CRISIS AND ITS MEANING

the enlightened classes of all nations a new conception of justice, a new ideal of human brotherhood, sooner or later to be carried into effect. But before speaking more explicitly of this, let us first inquire why it is that all the safeguards upon which we had relied to prevent war have failed us.

The Hague Tribunal has disappointed the high expectations that were at one time entertained as to the extension of its jurisdiction and its efficacy in preventing armed conflicts. It has indeed succeeded in settling a considerable number of minor questions that were causing friction, and might have developed into serious dimensions had they not been adjusted. But it is as illogical to argue that a tribunal like that at The Hague is competent to adjust major quarrels, brought about by great national ambitions, the lust for territory, the desire for continental or oceanic supremacy, as it would be to expect that a dam strong enough to keep a gentle stream within bounds will avail to hold back the torrents that rage at the time of melting snows. This device of an international court has been a disappointment because it is based on a false analogy. To many well-meaning people it seems the simplest thing in

THE WORLD CRISIS AND ITS MEANING

the world that quarrels between nations should be settled in a court of justice just as quarrels between individuals are settled. But the essential prerequisites of a court of justice are two. First that the judge shall be an impartial outsider and not a party in interest; secondly, that there shall be sufficient force at the disposal of the court to insure its judgment being obeyed. The force need not be actually employed, but it must exist in reserve, to be used in case of need. A court without power to give effect to its decisions is no court at all.

Now both these essential prerequisites are found in the case of controversies between individuals. When two citizens of New York are in litigation they are just two out of five millions, and it is a simple matter to find impartial judges. And the other prerequisite also is assured, the force necessary to give effect to the decisions of the court; it is the police force, backed by the public opinion of the five millions who are not at all interested in the particular differences of A and B, but are interested that A and B shall terminate their dispute without disturbing the security and peace of the town.

THE WORLD CRISIS AND ITS MEANING

In the case of the nations, precisely these two prerequisites are wanting. If there were a million nations, instead of half-a-dozen great powers that count, matters would stand differently. But suppose that the Dual Alliance and the Triple Entente were to bring their dispute before the Court at The Hague. Why, the judges to try the case would be Russians, Austrians, Germans, French, English—every one of them a party in interest, every one of them inevitably biased on one side or the other! Or let us imagine that the neutrals were asked to judge—Switzerland, the South American republics, even the United States; where would be the force to give effect to their decisions? Even the United States, impregnable as it is against aggression from without, would be powerless to transport a sufficient army across the seas to prevent the angry nations from rushing at each other's throats! And even if a special army could be constituted, adequate to support the judgment of the Court, an "international police force," as it is called, it would not be large enough to overpower the millions of troops that might be assembled by any one of the recalcitrant nations. Moreover, we should then have army against army, or

THE WORLD CRISIS AND ITS MEANING

armies. And that would not be the exercise of the police power; it would be full blown war called by another name.

The peace movement in general has proved ineffectual. Not many years ago a noble woman, the Baroness von Süttner, uttered a cry that seemed to ring through every civilized country. Out of the anguish of her own bitter experience, having lost her nearest male relatives in war, she rose like a prophesying sibyl, and in the name of womanhood, in the name of humanity she commanded, "Die Waffen nieder!" A merciful death just before the outbreak of the present war saved her from knowing how unavailing had been her cry. Also there was the attempted demonstration by writers like Jean Bloch and Norman Angell that war had become an impossibility. But was there ever more futile arithmetic? Was there ever a greater illusion than to suppose that war had become an illusion instead of remaining the most sinister and menacing of facts! We were told that universal bankruptcy would follow war; that the victor would be as greatly injured as the vanquished, his money being invested in the countries which he ravaged and his enemies being his customers. It was made

THE WORLD CRISIS AND ITS MEANING

clear that the great money kings upon whom it was supposed that the decision depended for war or peace, would never permit so great a piece of folly as war. But this legend of the absolute supremacy of the money power has been exploded. The great financiers, like others, have been affected by the war passion, or constrained by governmental pressure brought to bear upon them to furnish the very means for the business in hand.

The peace movement depended in the main on two appeals—the appeal to sentiment, to the horror of wounds and suffering, and the appeal to pecuniary self-interest. But both of these have proved insufficient. The crude idealists of force despise wounds, they glory in physical hardships, and take it as a sign of virility to inflict and to bear pain without wincing. And when furious passions are aroused the appeal to self-interest also does not work. An angry people, like an angry man, will shatter in a moment the edifice of prosperity and happiness which they have built up in years. The psychology of the peace movement has been mistaken. It took no account of the forces of human nature other than pity and self-interest, which have arisen like a flood and swept aside the feeble barriers placed in their way.

Religion, too, has proved to be a broken reed. It might have been expected that the teachings of the Prince of Peace would restrain the ferocities of his followers. Yet strange to say, religion has even exacerbated the warlike passion. In the name of Christ the soldiers of Russia were sent forth to slay the Christians of other lands. Lord Kitchener has supplied every private soldier with a tract, the first words of which are "Fear God and serve the King." Fear God by slaying the Germans! The German chancellor on his part says: "Let your hearts beat for God and your fists beat on the foe!" In every case the worship of God has been deemed consistent with hostility toward others equally called his children, and the word has gone forth: In the name of the God you fear and the Christ you love, kill!

Similarly international socialism, which was believed by many to be the safest insurance against international warfare, has disappointed the hopes that were founded upon it. Socialism attempted to divide the civilized world into two camps: labor on the one hand, and capital on the other—the lines that separate the nations being slurred over, if not obliterated. All the manual workers of the world were to be on the one side, as against the employers, the landed and industrial proprietors, on the other side. It was believed that in case of an issue arising between one political entity and another—France, Germany, England—the workers of one country would refuse to be led against their brother workers of other countries, the soldiers would strike, and war would thus be prevented. But when the situation which had been so long anticipated arose, the German workingman felt himself, after all, to be closer, more nearly related to the German capitalist than to the French workman across the frontier. "Deutschland, Deutschland über alles!"—Germany above everything, even above socialism! The socialists in the Reichstag, with the exception of a small minority, voted the war budget, and the millions of German socialists fell into line behind the flag. In Belgium Vandevelde, the socialist, entered the ministry. French socialists acted in the same manner. In England Ramsay MacDonald, who protested against the war, was compelled to resign the chairmanship of the Labor

THE WORLD CRISIS AND ITS MEANING

Party and the English laborers fell into line.

There was a force at work on which the socialists and the pacifists had not counted, a force which neither the increase of sympathy nor the desire for comfort had been able to extinguish, a force that triumphed over cosmopolitan brotherhood—the force of nationalism. The unbounded affirmation of nationalism is the ultimate cause of the struggle which we are witnessing. Militarism is but its instrument. We cannot overcome war by destroying militarism, because we cannot destroy militarism so long as the master motive of nationalism insists on availing itself of this tool. The mere private desire of a military caste for advancement would not be able to move the world if it were not that this motive is supported by forces working among the people themselves. Back of militarism is industrialism. The German Emperor is not the autocrat who presses the button; he is a spokesman of industrialism, which wants expansion, new markets, and of the nationalism of the whole people, which seeks to affirm itself in the face of the world. President Eliot has said that if only the people—they who have to bear the misery—had a chance, they would stop war.

THE WORLD CRISIS AND ITS MEANING

But the masses are full of the spirit of nationalism, and would rather bear their misery than forego the national aspiration. In truth, the uneducated think less of life than the more refined, and are the readier to engage in a quarrel and to kill or risk being killed. Besides, the monotony of their life is often so grievous that there is a welcome excitement in war.

It behoves us, then, to consider what is the right attitude towards nationalism. We must in the first place do justice to it. It will not do any longer to preach cosmopolitan brotherhood in defiance of these manifest, deeply-rooted patriotisms which, when unbridled, lead to such terrible excesses. How shall we efficiently bridle them? Nationalism at present is unpurified, unchastened, uncthicized. How shall its purification be achieved?

Nationalism has its source in the kinship we feel with those who use the same language, who observe the same manners and customs, who sing the same songs, who have the heritage of a common literature, a common history—in a word, who belong to the same type of human beings as ourselves. There are many types of humanity. You see a certain pattern worked out on a rug or a wall paper; you can follow the lines and the interweaving of the colors, their contrasts and their blendings. So there are certain mental patterns. Every one of the great nations represents a certain mental pattern of its own: certain ways of thinking about things, certain ways of feeling, a certain attitude towards life, a certain tincture of sentiment. The soul, the genius of one nation, is different from that of the others, the manners are different. The English lyric is unlike the German lyric. No great masterpiece of one literature has ever been successfully translated into another. It is especially language that distinguishes; a foreign idiom is a straitjacket—very few, even among educated persons, can express themselves freely in a language other than their own; they may be able to read a foreign language fluently, but when it comes to expressing their inmost thought, they feel more or less constrained. The wellspring of nationalism is the feeling of attraction towards those with whom we are at home, those who speak as we do, and who understand us when we speak, those whose minds bear imprinted upon them the same pattern as our own.

THE WORLD CRISIS AND ITS MEANING

Now, in the last hundred years, more or less, there has been a prodigious growth of nationalism in the world. The unification of Italy and of Germany, the national aspirations of the Greeks, the Slavs, the Czechs, are evidences of it. This development of the nationalistic principle has been due largely to the facilities of rapid communication which have brought into close and frequent touch members of the same stock formerly shut off from one another in particularistic seclusion. In former times patriotism was local, at best provincial. The different provinces of France had their own patriotisms. Each of the two hundred and thirty different German states had its particular patriotism; Germany was but an abstract name. So it was with Italy. In the age of railways, telegraphs and the press, the current of ideas and interests that flows in the capital reaches the remotest districts, a common life pulsates throughout the entire land. The value attached to the common mental pattern has thus been greatly enhanced. The average German of to-day is apt to feel that German culture and German civilization are the only kind worth having. They mean so much to him, why should they not mean everything to everyone?

THE WORLD CRISIS AND ITS MEANING

Why should they not obtain supremacy throughout the world? The French, the English, have the same feeling. "Anglo-Saxon supremacy," "the white man's burden" is the cry. Even the Slavs, who have not yet produced a great civilization of their own, are conscious of the potential gifts of a vigorous race, the Joseph among the nations, and they claim dominion for that which is inherent in them, that which is to be.

We are witnessing a vast struggle of the types of civilization with one another, each claiming superlative and exclusive value for itself, and therefore intolerant of the existence and claims of the others. Each of the great stocks that are at war is fighting for its supremacy in the belief that on its supremacy depends the existence of the mental pattern which it cherishes above all else—above peace, above pecuniary prosperity, above the life of the millions who are sacrificed in the conflict.

This, in my judgment, is the deepest of the causes of the world crisis. In the light of it we can understand the ruthlessness with which the war is conducted, and how the monstrous doctrine should arise that a nation is exempt from the obligation to be just to other nations;

THE WORLD CRISIS AND ITS MEANING

how the arch moral heresy should be propagated that morality is binding on individuals within a nation, but is without application to the conduct of one people toward other peoples. An English statesman was quoted as saying that "England could not exist if she were just a single day." Prince von Buelow exonerates England from the charge of perfidy so often brought against her, on the ground that she pursues implacably, relentlessly, her national interest, inasmuch as he believes that her example is one to be followed, not reprobated, by her rivals. In a recent number of the London *Spectator* a letter of the poet Wordsworth, written in 1811, is republished for the inspiration of the present generation of Englishmen. In it Wordsworth addresses himself to a writer who had advised the conquest of Italy by the British. He dissents from this writer to the extent of condemning conquest merely for the sake of conquest, but goes on to approve the subjection of Italy by British arms if it should be necessary to the existence and prosperity of the great and noble English nation. How strange a sentiment to come from the author of the "Ode to Duty"; how inexplicable, unless we remember the superlative value attributed by each of the nations to its own type of culture!

And yet it is so plain that no one type of civilization as yet achieved by any of the nations of the world is perfect or exclusive. They not only can and should exist side by side, but each requires the others to supplement its defects. Just as the crossing of rightly mated breeds leads to the evolution of higher offspring, so the crossing of civilizations will lead in time to higher and higher forms of civilization. This is the thought which seems most likely to cast a ray of light into the darkness wherein mankind is whelmed to-day. This is the teaching of which the nations and their leaders stand most in need. We have dwelt too long upon the cosmopolitan ideal of the likeness subsisting underneath the differences that distinguish men from one another. We must insist as we have never yet done on respect for the differences themselves, on the right of men and of nations to be unlike ourselves, on our obligation not only to tolerate but to welcome the differences, recognizing their fruitful interdependence and seeking to achieve their eventual harmony. This is the new conception of human brotherhood, without which war and the preparations for war will not cease.

The world to-day is at fault, not only in respect to ethical conduct, but in respect to ethical ideals. I would not be understood as countenancing the deep pessimism which has settled on certain minds: it is not true that no moral progress has been achieved, that civilization is a thin veneer, and that the brute in man has in no respect been tamed. Such expressions as these are the petulant outbursts of a disappointed optimism. There *has* been moral progress, as is exemplified by the greater respect shown to woman, whose position has never been so high as it is at the present day, and in the finer regard for childhood and its rights, and in other ways. There is no incident to-day to match the sack of Rome by the Constable of Bourbon in 1527, and the world is improving even in the conduct of war. But the codes we get from the bibles do not adequately help, nor do the systems of the closet philosophers. We need new moral concepts. The war is a demonstration of the insufficiency of our ethical concepts. Humanity is in the birth-throes of new moral ideals. What may be called man-to-man morality has been enhanced. But the morality of people *versus* people has hardly yet been sketched. The difference between individual ethics and the principles upon which international morality should be based has not been worked out. And here a great field is open; a world-wide ethical movement is called for. For ideas are forces. They are not competent to move men, and to alter the conduct of mankind, without the aid of impulse and feeling. But neither do impulse and feeling avail without the control and direction supplied by great ideas.

I have challenged the notion that an international court of justice can either pass impartial judgments on major points under existing conditions, or secure the observance of its decrees unless these are backed up by force. But the force necessary to make the Hague Tribunal a genuine court of international justice will come into being in the shape of an enlightened public opinion, according as each nation becomes aware that the nationalism of one people is consistent with that of others. There must be created throughout the world, not the belief in an individualistic cosmopolitan brotherhood such as the peace movement has hitherto advocated, but a deep sense of the worth of

THE WORLD CRISIS AND ITS MEANING

the different types of civilization, and the need of each to be complemented by the rest.

A long course of education lies ahead. I will mention one point at which the educative process might properly begin. This is the colonial policy of European nations. In the treatment of the Oriental peoples and the backward races all the European nations have adopted the rule of exploitation. A cry of indignation has gone up, and justly, because Germany, the strong nation, trampled under foot the rights of Belgium, the weaker nation. The defense that necessity knows no law cannot be accepted. But every one of the European nations has followed exactly the same line of conduct, the strong trampling upon the weak in the East and in Africa. It is only three years since Sir Edward Grey, then and now the Foreign Minister of England, combined with Russia to strangle Persia—the land that gave the noble religion of Zoroaster to the world, the land of Omar Khayyam and Firdusi, a land in which had developed a promising movement toward democratic freedom. The corrupt Shah had been expelled, parliamentary government had been established, and with the assistance of the young American, Mr. Shuster, Persia

THE WORLD CRISIS AND ITS MEANING

was beginning to establish order in its financial administration, when all this life of a resurrected people was mercilessly crushed in order that British interests in India might be safeguarded! Where then was respect for the weak nation shown by the strong? Where then was the champion of international righteousness? Germany was guilty in like manner in Kiau Chou, both in its seizure of territory and in the methods adopted. France was pushing its egotistical interests in Morocco, in Tunis and in Indo-China. And Belgium herself—bleeding, victimized Belgium—can we, with all our sympathy for her present suffering, forget that it was Belgian capital, leagued with the Belgian king, that enacted the nightmare of atrocities on the Congo at which the world stood aghast seven years ago? There is not one of these nations that comes into court with clean hands. There is not one that has not been guilty in its dealings with the Oriental peoples and the backward races. If I were a believer in the old-time notion of retribution, I should say that the judgment of God has come upon them, that they have sown the wind out there, and are reaping the whirlwind at home. In one sense there has been such retribution.

THE WORLD CRISIS AND ITS MEANING

The contempt of the strong for the weak, the methods of violence which have been used outside of Europe, are now being employed by the peoples of Europe against one another.

Right here, then, is the first step in education. A new colonial policy should be enforced; not Persia for British India, but Persia for the welfare of the Persians, and China for the Chinese, and Africa for the people of Africa. If the people of Europe can be taught to respect different types of civilization, or potential civilization, in other lands, they will thus be trained to respect the national ideals and types of civilization of their immediate neighbors.

We in America are in a position to bring home this great lesson. When the time of settlement comes this plea for a new colonial policy, in my view, should be our counsel. And we shall have the right to speak this word, because we have been true to our faith in Cuba, we have resisted the temptation to disturb the integrity of Mexico, and we are preparing to give full expression to the policy of "The Philippines for the Filipinos."

II

MILITARISM AND ITS EULOGISTS

RECENTLY, in one of the Sunday newspapers, an artist sought to figure Belgium mourning over her dead. It was the conventional conception: a woe-begone woman representing Belgium, and in her lap the head of a fallen soldier. One could not but be struck with the inadequacy of convention in this case to express the truth. For it is the boundlessness of this war that impresses and overwhelms us, the manifoldness and vastness of the woe, incapable of being personified in a single figure. If a painter were to portray masses of men mowed down together, ditches in which a thousand dead are lowered; if he could represent a whole countryside devastated, he would still furnish only a photograph, and not a picture. No one has ever painted the Alps or the boundless sea; no one can paint this war and the horror of it, and such grandeur as there is amid the horror of it.

MILITARISM AND ITS EULOGISTS

The last statement will be challenged resentfully by some. War, it will be said, is just butchery; it is a shameful blot on civilization; it is the accursed thing. It is to be anathematized. There should be no parleying with its fancied grandeurs. Immanuel Kant wrote a much-quoted treatise entitled "A Proposal for Perpetual Peace." And endued as his mind was with philosophic calm beyond the gift of most philosophers he nevertheless breaks into passionate language in speaking of the barbarities of war. He describes the European nations as "European savages." He compares them to cannibals, with this difference, that while cannibals devour their enemies, the European nations seek to reduce theirs to a condition of servitude in order to increase their own power. By the way, he also ridicules the attempt to insure peace by armed preparation for war in words which might have been written to-day.

Such sentiments as these are common to most of our pacifists. But many militarists, both those abroad and those of this country, take a decidedly different view. However we may account for it, a strong military party exists in the United States, working for the most part secretly, but sometimes, as at present, much in evidence. The arguments used by them are of two kinds. War, according to them, is indispensable to prevent mankind from sinking into sloth and ease and materialism; it is the soil, drenched indeed with blood, in which, and in which alone, flourish the most splendid virtues. This is also von Moltke's view. Perpetual peace, he says, is a dream, and not even a beautiful dream. Another argument is, that although peace would be preferable, a lasting and righteous peace for any nation has been hitherto unattainable and therefore we must increase our armaments.

Let us give due attention to the apologists for war. The pacifists' attack on militarism has time and time again been repulsed. With all their outcry, they have not made the impression which they expected to make. Is not this due, in part at least, to the fact that they have underestimated the strength of their opponents? Lincoln wisely said that in meeting an adversary in debate it is not only the part of fairness, but of sound policy, to state his case as strongly as he could state it himself, more strongly if possible than he would. If you can vanquish him at the points where he is strong-

MILITARISM AND ITS EULOGISTS

est, he is definitely defeated. Let us endeavor to follow this counsel and ask what are the strongest arguments on behalf of militarism.

One of the reasons why war has been praised discloses itself to us as we read the Homeric poems, especially the Iliad. Through the Iliad runs a high festive strain, celebrating the glorious deeds of heroes. The trumpet notes in it predominate. But under it runs a minor melody, a plaintive strain. The hosts of Greece and the armies of Priam meet on the windy plain of Troy somewhat like figures in a mist. They form, they encounter, they recede, they are dissolved. Achilles speaks of himself pathetically as wondering at the strange fatality that sent him to vex the Trojans. It is all a kind of fatality. The narrator does not take decidedly the side of his countrymen, but lavishes some of the most exquisite touches of his pencil on Hector, the hero-adversary of his people. The struggle is essentially purposeless, and it is the futility of life that weighs upon the soul of Homer. The world-conception which forms the background of his poem is essentially sad. The generations of men fall like leaves, and therefore battle and physical valor are cherished as means of shaking off the tedium of existence, as means of self-intoxication, and also as means of lifting man in his own esteem, which the dead weight of fate depresses. For the moment, at any rate, the warrior has a sense of personal value, as with mighty arm he vanquishes his opponent. And he may even hope that his deeds, if sufficiently illustrious, will be embalmed in the songs of bards, and still admired by a distant posterity.

The question, What is it that makes life worth while? is asked in every age. The answer given by the Greeks in the time when the Homeric poems were composed was: To give immediate expression to one's personality in physical valor; to accentuate one's selfhood by prevailing over foes. Life is a great struggle to think well of ourselves. The greatest evil is neither poverty nor sickness, but self-contempt. Get into action, do something, and at least for the time being you stand up large in your own esteem; and physical valor and prowess are the cheapest and readiest means of thus expressing personality. The *tedium vitæ,* the desire to escape from the monotony of life, is still one of the fruitful causes that lead to the exaltation of war. It is not so much the externals, the nodding plumes, the glint of steel, the brilliant uniforms, the drum's alarum, the clarion music —urging the spirit to mount and the line to sweep forward. These have their effect chiefly as concomitants. The desire to break away from a commonplace existence takes a foremost place amongst other appeals to bring thousands to the recruiting stations to-day.

Again both the moralist and the militarist agree that this physical existence of ours is not to be valued on its own account, but is to be counted as a tool which the spirit shall use as a means to an end; and that life may be cast away lightly if the preservation of the means should conflict with the end which it is intended to subserve. We must agree with moralist and militarist that mere living is worthless—vegetative, sordid living, plethoric with the baser satisfactions. Life is desirable only when filled with noble content—an earthen vessel when filled with golden wine. But we differ as to the kind of content with which the vessel shall be filled. Right here is the source of error into which some of the greatest minds have been seduced, and which has led them to eulogize war.

Aristotle is one of these greatest minds, the chief of the ancient philosophers. As a thinker he was perhaps incomparable. His gigantic intellect impressed itself upon mankind to such an extent that for two thousand years he ruled the schools. But as a personality he was, if possible, greater still—a clear-cut, commanding figure; noble, clean, if also severe. In his book on Ethics he represents courage in battle as the highest of the moral virtues—not the courage evinced on the sick-bed which we should be tempted to rate higher, not the silent fortitude of those who, like the victims of the *Titanic* disaster, go down at sea, but precisely the courage manifested in giving and receiving wounds, in dealing death and frankly meeting it. There must be an excuse for the fight, some worthy cause for the sake of which life is thrown away; but given the cause, then the mere act of sacrificing the physical life betrays in him who does it a magnanimous soul, a soul that puts the earthly existence in its proper place as subordinate to something loftier in man. In Aristotle's view, life is worth while *according to what you see.* You can live on a low level or on a high one. If on the latter, using your eye of reason, then you behold an object of contemplation fairer than the fair, wiser than the wise, the everlasting ever-felicitous Godhead, the uncreated Being. If you are

MILITARISM AND ITS EULOGISTS

a citizen of the upper level you will think little of the physical life; whether it comes or goes will matter little, and you will show your nativity in the higher realm just by the fact that you are ready to dismiss your physical life, as a child would kick away a ball, as of no serious account. The mere willingness on a proper occasion to treat life as a bauble or an incumbrance to be laid aside, as on its own account a thing only to be loftily despised, is the signature of the superior personality. This contempt of mere existence is the distinguishing trait of the soldier as the philosopher conceives him. This it is that makes his action beautiful and commends him to fame and glory. Many others have followed Aristotle in this view. And the work of the soldier has undoubtedly not been without this redeeming trait.

The Stoics also, with their doctrine of self-mastery, had no disapproval for the virtues of war. Marcus Aurelius wrote his *Meditations* in a soldier's camp. Further, of the two ideas of order and progress, the first was dominant in the Stoic philosophy and the second not apparent at all. Marcus Aurelius the emperor drew his sword to maintain the established order of the civilized world comprised in the Roman Empire against barbarian attacks from without—just as he used violence to suppress the Christians, whom he believed to imperil the internal security of the state.

Nor must we omit reference to the attitude of the early Christians towards bloodshed. It is peculiar and interesting. They were, of course, opposed to shedding the blood of others, but they gloried in *having their own blood shed* for the sake of the faith. Unwilling to use violence, they yet desired the crown of martyrdom, which they must suffer violence to obtain. They would have agreed with Aristotle, as do we, that the physical life is not worth while on its own account, but only as the instrument of some higher use to which it may be put, and that when the continuation of physical existence is in conflict with the higher purpose, the former must give way. They would disagree with Aristotle, as should we, as to what that higher purpose is.

After the *tedium vitæ,* and the contempt for mere existence, a third source from which springs the magnifying of war is the idea of honor. Honor is a class notion. Every social class has its own code of honor—the physicians, the lawyers, the merchants, the military class.

MILITARISM AND ITS EULOGISTS

The idea of honor is connected with the specific virtue which a class is expected to practice. Thus the honor of the merchant as a merchant consists in solvency. Insolvency, even when due to misfortune, and without blame, is felt by sensitive merchants as a stain to be purged by the payment of debts, even after the lapse of years. The honor of the merchant is to practice that virtue upon which the security of mercantile transactions depends, that virtue which is exacted of his class. Though they are akin, there is a distinction between honor and honesty, since honor is found in practicing the specific virtues of one's class. It may be the peculiar honor of the merchant to pay his debts. But this is not the honor of the aristocrat. In English novels there is constant reference, without strict condemnation, to noble lords who do not pay their debts to tradesmen. The great Pitt died with thousands of pounds of debt unpaid.

Now, the honor of the soldier consists in the exhibition of courage. Cowardice is his disgrace. A fighter is expected to be brave, to seek danger rather than avoid it, to be quick to draw, slow to sheathe his sword, so that the quality in which his honor shines may not be

39

questioned. Military honor is sensitive because bravery needs to be incessantly vindicated, that it may not become suspect. He who is brave under one set of circumstances might be found weak in another; he who is bold to encounter one antagonist might quail before another and more formidable adversary. Hence the practice of dueling. The typical militarist, where honor is at stake, finds occasion for a quarrel "in a straw." To our American common-sense notions there appears to be no credible connection between an insult and successful sword or pistol practice on the author of the affront. What an adversary says may even be true. How does the fact that I wound him or kill him shake the truth of his assertion? But from the militarist point of view the matter stands differently. To insult a military officer is to cast a doubt on his reputation for courage. Who would venture to affront him if his willingness and ability to use his weapon were beyond possible dispute? Therefore he must fight in order to rehabilitate his honor, for his honor and courage are accounted to be the same thing.

The idea of military honor has an absurd, and also a nobler, aspect. It gave birth to the

MILITARISM AND ITS EULOGISTS

virtues of chivalry among Saladin's knights, in Medieval Europe and in Japan. Chivalry is marked by exquisite courtesy toward equals— that is, toward men as sensitive to the point of honor as oneself. It is distinguished by a proud disdain to measure oneself against those who are weaker, and, in its best examples, by devout service to women. Bayard "fearless and stainless" in France, and Sir Philip Sydney in England, are perhaps the most attractive characters that chivalry has produced: Bayard, who held the bridge alone against two hundred Spaniards, who with a handful defended Mézières against 35,000 foes, who knighted his sovereign, who protected the ladies of the Château against insult; Sir Philip Sydney, who, suffering from burning thirst himself, passed the cup of water to a wounded soldier with the well-known words: "Thy need is greater than mine." Not really that his need was greater, but that the soldier was probably less potent than the knightly Sydney to forego his need. It is these chivalric virtues, the threatened decay of which in modern society De Tocqueville fears and deplores in his book on "Democracy in America." And it is because war is believed to be indispensable to the production of such virtues that many of its advocates assert the continued necessity of war, despite the actual miseries which it produces and which they fully admit and acknowledge.

What reply have we to offer to the pleas thus far made? First, there is a canker in these roses of chivalry, a flaw in these virtues. They are all self-regarding, and no virtue is truly worth the name unless it includes on equal terms the interests of fellowmen. Neither egoism nor altruism is moral, neither self-regarding nor other-regarding action, but solely that kind of conduct which combines inseparably the interests of the self and the other. Now the chivalrous man acts according to *Hamlet's* command to *Polonius* with respect to the treatment of the players. Chivalry asks: How is it becoming that I should act in view of the distinction that belongs to me as a knight or a gentleman? The chivalrous man bestows charity on the poor, not primarily because the needs of the poor man require his attention, but inasmuch as it is proper for the gentleman to be bountiful toward the wretched. The chivalrous man protects woman, not primarily because of the transfiguring soul which he sees in physically feebler womanhood, but because it is

MILITARISM AND ITS EULOGISTS

proper for powerful man to take upon himself the service of the weak. The two points of view are not, indeed, in practice as sharply separable as I have here set them down, but yet the egoistic, self-regarding element in chivalry prevails. Hence its gross shortcomings; hence the fact that while some women were selected for homage, and even mystical devotion, the position of women as a whole was deplorable. While some were protected, others were cast to the wolves, the unbridled passions of men.

This is the first serious point of criticism. But a criticism of still greater importance is this: If we undertake to judge of war we should judge on the ground of its principal effects, and not on the ground of its incidental effects, its by-products. All the virtues that have been so highly praised are *by-products*. The main effects are wholly evil—the intrinsic effects, those which it is in the nature of war as a phenomenon of human behavior to produce. This is a point of the utmost importance, and yet one that is constantly overlooked. Even gambling might be justified on the ground of the incidentally valuable qualities which it tends to produce; for instance, self-control, ability to suppress the most violent feelings—despair, hope, exultation—beneath the mask of utter indifference. The gambler also is often generous with his gains. I venture to think one can obtain larger gifts for the poor from those who have the gambling spirit than from the thrifty. Their motto is: Live and let live. But the main effect of gambling is disintegrating to character and degrading to the last degree. The venal politician may be mentioned as another instance. The venal politician of the slums is kind to the poor; he provides for their needs in winter, helps them to escape when in difficulties. There is a kind of good fellowship bred by his trade. But is a system the purpose of which is to subordinate the public good to the pecuniary profit of "the organization" any the less infamous on that account?

The accumulation of fortunes by reprehensible means, which we have witnessed in the United States, in like manner has thrown off certain perilously alluring by-products: institutions for the combating of disease managed on the most scientific principles, endowments of research, pensions for teachers, and the like. Certainly the public cannot fail to take note of these benefactions, and cannot do otherwise

MILITARISM AND ITS EULOGISTS

than acknowledge their beneficence. And in passing judgment on the benefactions it would be contrary to every finer feeling to impugn the motives of the donors. Good and evil are strangely mingled in our human clay, and it is quite possible for those who have done great evil in one direction to be genuinely inclined towards doing great good in other directions. All the same, it would be the greatest possible mistake to refrain from plainly and strongly condemning the methods which have been pursued in achieving these formidable accumulations. The benefactions are incidental, and might possibly have been achieved in other ways. The methods used are intrinsically pernicious. And precisely the same applies to war. That there are certain admirable qualities developed by it we need not deny—although these are not only incidental but exceptional. The feudal soldiery were not all Bayards or Sydneys; far from it. Pillage, licentiousness, cruelty, mark the track of the armies that marched across European countries. But aside from all this we must distinguish between the product and the by-product. It seems almost incredible that minds like von Moltke and the great thinkers I have mentioned should not have made this distinction. We at least should be under no illusion in this respect. All that is best in the life and institutions of mankind is the work of the social spirit. War intrinsically, in its very nature, involves the unloosing of the anti-social forces.

But right here has been advanced a new plea in favor of war, based upon the conditions of modern life, which, as concerning closely the attitude of the American people on this subject, it will be well for us to consider. There is a new situation now in the world; the reign of commercialism has set in. We are given over, it is said, to the pursuit of wealth and material ease. We are in danger of being suffocated in plenty, or at least of being infected and poisoned, by the desire for material abundance. War is needed as a tonic, as a means of sanitation, of rousing the slothful to endurance of hardship, of reducing the insubordinate to discipline. Once again certain incidental effects produced by war are lifted up into the major place and are allowed to obscure the permanent and intrinsic results of it.

To meet this argument it will suffice to point out that like other tonics this particular one is temporary in its effect and is followed by reaction. Take even such a war as the Civil War, in which the floodgates of moral enthusiasm were opened wide. We cannot escape observing either the tremendous impetus given to speculation during the war, or the passion for material aggrandizement in all directions that followed it. Again, the reign of materialism that set in in Germany after the highwater mark of idealistic enthusiasm for national unity had subsided is an instance in point. I happened to be in Berlin during and after the Franco-German war, and I remember well the kind of vertigo that seized upon the people after the payment of the French indemnity. The defeat for France was no less a defeat for what was best in the German soul!

To meet this argument further: even if war could be trusted to idealize a nation's aims, surely we are not shut up to the alternative of materialism or war. If we should discard the fierce stimulant of war which for a season sends the energies up to their highest pitch and then allows them to decline, there are in the daily life of a civilized people enough possible intensive spurs to strenuousness. In the pursuit of science and art, in the disinterested impulses that are called into play in social reform, in the callings of the teacher, of the physician—there are a thousand appeals that can elicit motives and inspire actions fit to raise men above the base sphere of material desire into far nobler regions and keep them there.

It is true that the idealism created for the time being by war, however temporary it may be, however lamentable the after results, has one great incontestable merit, in that it brings home to every citizen the obligation he owes to his nation in its collective capacity, and to the things for which his nation stands. It is true, on the other hand, that the coast-guard who leaps into the sea to save a drowning man risks or sacrifices his life only for individuals; that the locomotive engineer who puts his life in jeopardy to save those of the passengers on his train sacrifices himself only for individuals; so does the physician, so does the teacher serve the individual—while the millions who to-day are marching to battlefields are offering their lives for a great, collective personality, for something as much greater than the individuals as the Niobe group is greater than the hand or limb of one of its component figures. The national ideal is like a work of art. The nation does not exist for its individuals, their prosperity or so-called happiness; the individuals exist to contribute, and their real prosperity and happiness consist in contributing to the perfection of that work of art which we call the nation's ideal. I must and do admit, therefore, that patriotism produces a greater spiritual uplift than the life-saving of individuals. War does call out self-sacrifice for the sake of the nation, for something vaster than the individual; it demands sacrifice for the existence of a people and the ideals for which a people stands; and nothing can bring home the consciousness of obligation towards these so effectively as sacrifice on their behalf. This is the strongest argument on behalf of war.

But what I do not and cannot admit is that this kind of worship and service of the thing divine, a nation's ideals, cannot be rendered better in peace than war. It is a hateful nationalist orthodoxy, borrowed from an obsolete religious orthodoxy, which declares that a nation must be washed in another nation's blood in order that it may be saved. What we may not admit is that in order to be true artists of our nation's ideal, we must first of all arm ourselves with clubs and break in pieces all the statuary that is being perfected in our neighbors' workshops. Let it be our national ideal, in the course of human evolution, to bring to birth on this continent a new type of human being, as far above the present type as this is above the cave man, and to do this by means of the power and influence of free institutions. If this be our national ideal, and not the mere pursuit of lucre, then I am certain that we can have it brought home to us far more clearly and effectively in peace than in war. The place to bring it home should be in our municipal councils, in our primaries, at the polls, in our legislatures—in a word, in our political life and conduct. The object of our politics should be precisely the realizing of this national ideal. If our politics be dominated by this conception— the politics of the legislator in the legislative chamber equally with the politics of the voter in the booth—so that all work together to find means of perfecting the national ideal and winning all to share in its realization, then we shall find the days of peace to serve our end better than days of war.

There remains one more plea which must be in part conceded to the advocates of war. There is such a thing as a just war, a war in defense of a nation's existence against unjust aggres-

MILITARISM AND ITS EULOGISTS

sion. If we do not admit this, we shall have to put a stain on the memory of Washington; we shall have to reverse the judgment of mankind in regard to those who fought at Marathon and Salamis, the Switzers who defended successfully the freedom of the mountains against Austrian invasion, the Belgians who have defended their independence against German aggression. As the world stands to-day it may still be necessary, even for us, at some time to enter into the lists and to wage what may rightly be called a holy war. But in making this concession we are at the very opposite pole from the militarist champions of war. The grounds on which we put the concession constitute in themselves the most stringent condemnation of war in general, and are most apt to prevent the circumstances arising in which a permissible war could occur. The champions of militarism tell us first that war is a good thing, a necessary tonic, a means of breeding virtues —the by-product being taken for the product— and secondly that it is necessary to make ample preparation for war on grounds of national self-defense. And each of the arguments is used to reënforce the other, like two playing cards which cannot stand unless they lean upon one another. Now, we say war is a hideous thing, evil in itself, but that sometimes it may become necessary to save a nation's very existence, because of the evil in others who seek to violate a nation's rights. Well, then, say the militarists, where is the difference? But the difference is absolute. It consists in the great ethical conception which we should take as our guide in these tangled, fearful situations, a conception which is lacking on the side of the champions of force; the ethical conception that our nation's rights are indissolubly bound up with the rights of other nations—are like a stone in a mosaic of rights, are like a living branch on the tree of rights; and that we cannot justly defend our rights save as we bear in mind and sedulously protect in our thought, and seek to safeguard in our action, the rights complementary to our own, the true rights of the aggressors themselves.

Self-defense has generally meant standing up for one's own rights. But anyone who stands up for his rights, who separates in mind his right from the correlative right of the other party, will inevitably glide over from right into might. He will begin by exercising right and presently change to the exercise of mere might.

The only possible way to defend ourselves from that is to bear in mind that our right is an organ in the organism of rights. The great ethical error of the world till now has been that in righteous self-defense men have become most unrighteous, because in self-defense they have thought of their right as sundered from the right of others. Yet my right is but one blade of the shears, and the right of my fellow, even though he be the aggressor, is the other blade.

The attitude thus indicated should determine the spirit of self-defense in the case of individuals, of social classes, and of peoples. An individual may be attacked by one who in a fit of passion attempts to kill him. It is then the duty of the individual to defend himself. It would be immoral in him to practice the policy of non-resistance. He should not only protect the humanity that resides in his own person, but should also protect the humanity that resides in the person of the aggressor. He should prevent if he can the latter from perpetrating a crime, and save him from losing to that extent his character as a human being.

Again, in the conflicts of laborers and employers, the defense of rights on either side should be regulated by the same principle. Laborers protest that their employer has been unjust, oppressive. They combine to defend their rights, and in this they are justified. But often the movement of protest, which began with a strike on behalf of right, degenerates into sheer assertion of might. The labor organization, if sufficiently strong, becomes dictatorial, peremptory, formulates demands inconsistent with sound business and with the self-respect of the employer. Now so long as the present industrial system continues, so long as there are employers, the employers have certain rights, because they have certain functions. Unduly to restrict their functions is to destroy their rights. Conversely, the employer may begin by resisting the tyranny of labor, and in so far as he does this we approve of his action. But presently, in defending his rights, he is apt wholly to forget the rights existing on the opposite side, in particular the indispensable right of association. He announces his intention to crush the union of laborers, and thus in his blind assertion of the fractional right which is his, he destroys the integral right which is compounded of his and theirs.

In the war of the nations waged in Europe at present, we see the absence of the principle,

MILITARISM AND ITS EULOGISTS

and the fatal consequences of its absence illustrated on the largest scale. Each of the great nations, according to its own view, is defending its rights. The Germans are fighting for their sacred culture, the Slavs are shedding their blood for Slavism, the English for the maintenance of the British Empire and its institutions. None of them consider the correlative rights of their neighbors. Not one of them thinks of its right as a branch on a tree of rights. We listen with heavy hearts to their several pleas. We realize that each of them is in earnest and righteous in its own eyes, but we realize also how deficient the notion of right still is in the minds of the civilized nations and of their rulers.

Military preparation is just now being strongly pressed upon the attention of the American public. We must prepare, it is said, to defend ourselves against possible aggressors. To do so, we must increase our armaments and train our young men in the use of deadly weapons. To what extent we must do so in order to be actually prepared is a technical question which we need not discuss. But here, too, the spirit in which self-defense is undertaken, or prospectively regarded, is everything. Someone has said that we are the kind of nation that will not do wrong to any foreign people, and will not suffer wrong at the hands of any other people. Our history, alas! does not wholly bear out the former assertion. But if we are indeed resolved not to be aggressors upon foreign rights, there is little likelihood that we shall become the objects of foreign aggression. Also, in defending our rights, if we are ever put to it, we must distinguish sharply between rights and interests. The two are too often confounded. Our interests in the Pacific, for instance, are one thing. Our rights in Asia are a totally different matter. Our rights there are strictly limited by the rights of the peoples of Asia.

Here again let us adopt the spirit of Lincoln. Though in fact the president of the North, Lincoln was in spirit throughout his administration the president of the whole country. He ever kept in view the rights of those who, for the time being, were aggressors. He believed that the destruction of the Union would be an injury to the seceding states as well as to the loyal. He believed that the extinction of slavery would be an untold blessing to the South, as indeed it has proved to be. He fought secession not to crush the seceders, but to win them back, with malice toward none, with charity—that is, with largest consideration—for all. It is in this spirit alone that a righteous war should be waged.

III

AMERICAN IDEALS CONTRASTED WITH GERMAN AND ENGLISH

MANY of our fellow-citizens of German birth, aside from the profound anxiety descendants of all the nationalities now at war naturally feel for friends at the front, are troubled with a new misgiving as to their own place in the American nation. They are asking themselves whether the people of this country are really the American people, or are rather an Anglo-American people. They are asking whether the English element is so much the dominant factor in the Republic that persons of different origin are, as it were, citizens of an inferior grade. Politically, of course, the rights of all are secured by fundamental enactments. But rights may be secured on parchment, and the franchise freely exercised at the polls, while actual equality is denied.

The reason for this misgiving is plain. Public opinion in the United States is decisively

AMERICAN, GERMAN AND ENGLISH IDEALS

on the side of the Allies, and this practically means on the side of England. France is known to traveling Americans and to our artists, who love her, but very little to the general public. The presence of Russia on the same side as England is an element of weakness rather than strength in the cause of the Allies. England is the magnet that has caused public sentiment to swerve to the side of the Triple Entente. And from this it is but a step to infer that the sympathies enlisted on the side of England are due to racial memories, ancient attachments, ties of kinship.

Put in this broad fashion, the inference is certainly erroneous. We may recall that during the Boer War the sympathies of the United States were largely anti-English. Partisanship on the side of the Allies or of England in this present war is undoubtedly due to a judgment of right and wrong. It is believed that right is on one side and wrong on the other. We need not here enter into the debate. But the misgiving to which I have alluded does suggest a very important inquiry, namely, whether and to what extent the foreign-born citizen may be expected to divest himself of his character as an alien and clothe himself, as it were, with a new personality. And if the immigrant in crossing the sea is to suffer a sea-change, how deep should it go?

It is true that every country is in a certain sense the motherland of America. There are Swedes here and Danes; there are Germans, Russians, Irish, Italians, French. Twenty-three languages are spoken in one of our public schools. Many countries have contributed in various proportions toward the population of New York and of this country. And yet, must not the foreign-born, be he German or French or what-not, face the fact that in a certain sense England is peculiarly the mother country of America? The relations of the people of the United States with England are in some respects closer than with the inhabitants of other European countries. A common language is a great bond. Language is not a mere external thing. It is the instrument used by the mind to express itself. We may pour fluid metal into one mold or another, but the metal will take on the shape of the mold; so the thought takes on the characteristics of the language in which it is expressed. And English is the language of the United States. It has been and it will be; there must be a common language if there is

AMERICAN, GERMAN AND ENGLISH IDEALS

to be a united nation, and there is no other language that has the least chance to expel the English in this country from its supremacy. Nor need we lament that this is so. The English language is rich and flexible, made capable of exquisite shading by a long succession of great literary artists, and it is still growing and capable of new creations. No one can expect to live in America without habitually employing the English speech, and in so doing his mental habits are inevitably affected. He necessarily suffers a certain "sea-change."

Again, English common law is the basis of American law. English political institutions as brought over to this country are the stock from which our own institutions have developed. This constitutes another close bond.

But now for the other side! A mere bird's-eye glance at the superficies of American life, and of those political institutions the germ of which was imported from abroad, suffices to produce a profound impression of novelty. We need but compare the American presidency, with its fixed term of incumbency irrespective of the change of parties, with English cabinet government, or examine the functions of the United States Supreme Court, or contrast our

Senate with the House of Lords, in order to realize that the two developments, the English and American, though united at their origin, have since widely diverged. The American nation is really a new and distinctive nation, and not merely a branch of Anglo-Saxondom. But new and distinctive in what respect? Surely in the presence and operation amongst us of a new ideal of life, differing from that of other peoples—a new American ideal, which may be contrasted, for instance, with the German and English ideals. Let me enlarge upon this contrast, in order to bring out the difference.

By the ruling ideal I mean especially that which has to do with the standard by which the place of a man in the social scale is determined; the grounds on which he rises or descends in social esteem, and more or less in his own esteem.

There are, of course, certain general standards of evaluation which prevail the world over which here may be taken for granted. In every society men of wealth, rightly or wrongly, enjoy greater social prestige than poor men. The world over, personal charm, affability, courteous manners, etc., count. But these are universal credentials. What we are here concerned

AMERICAN, GERMAN AND ENGLISH IDEALS

with are the peculiar national standards. As the different nations have different standards for measuring things, such as the pint and the liter, the meter and the yard, so different peoples have different measures for determining the value of a man. And these national standards let in light on the deeper tendencies that move in a nation's life.

The German ideal, roundly speaking, is that of efficiency. The social value of a man is determined by his occupation, his task, and the measure of his proficiency in it. There are lower and higher tasks. There is the occupation of the laborer, the artisan, the merchant, the university professor, the king. In Germany a man counts according to the dignity of his task and his ability in the performance of it.

The system of titles prevailing in any country, or the absence of any, is a most interesting index of national psychology. In England there are very high-sounding titles, but observe that they stop short just above the middle class. In France there is a shadow remaining of the titular system in the decorations of the Legion of Honor. In the United States there are no titles—a point on which we shall dwell later. But in Germany the titles run vertically from the top almost to the lowest stratum. Above the indiscriminate proletariat almost everyone has a title. Why is this? For the reason that a man's title refers to his occupation, to the work he does; and the occupation determines how he is rated, the degree to which he counts. The titles of nobility were originally derived from the military occupation. The physician, when he has attained a certain eminence in his profession, is entitled *Medicinalrath*. The merchant is decorated with the title of *Kommercienrath*. Then there is the *Finanzrath*, the *Justizrath*. But it is important to remark that further down the same method is still in use. The builder is called *Herr Baumeister*, the engineer *Herr Ingenieur*. Even the janitor expects to be addressed as *Herr Hausmeister*. The title is that which entitles a man, or indicates the degree to which a man is entitled, to social consideration. And the fact that the title is elaborately spread out on the address of letters, is engraved even on the tombstone after a man is dead—the title which designates the occupation—is evidence of the intimate connection upon which I am laying stress, in analyzing the psychology of the German ideal, between the task and personal value.

AMERICAN, GERMAN AND ENGLISH IDEALS

The matter of efficiency needs to be further defined by two determining factors. The German people, as everyone acknowledges, are a highly intellectual people. Their peculiar kind of efficiency is the fruit of the invariable combination of theory and practice on which they lay such stress, the intellectual penetration of every task. They do not rely as much as others do on knack, ingenuity, or rule of thumb. They investigate with minute patience the scientific conditions that underlie every practical problem. They base work on science. They endeavor to think out beforehand every step of the process. It is for this reason, for example, that they have taken the lead in the chemical industry. It is said that in one of the great chemical works on the Rhine several hundred chemists are constantly employed in the laboratories conducted by the firm. It is the same in minor occupations. Germany is covered with a network of vocational schools for tailors, carpenters, bricklayers, plumbers and barbers, all having for their object to train those who are employed in these occupations in such scientific principles as may be of use to them in the performance of their daily work.

The second factor that determines the German conception of work, and of efficiency in work, is discipline—not the discipline of an external force imposed upon the worker, but a call to which he is expected to respond of his own accord. The task lays certain obligations upon him who would perform it well. To rise to these obligations is discipline. Laboriousness, punctuality, patient endurance of fatigue, persistence, suppression of the play instinct, the overcoming of inertia and of the tendency to wander off in thought during the hours of work —these are among his ever-present conscious duties. The idea of the obligation laid upon the worker by his task is the essence, as I understand it, of that great though perhaps narrow conception of *Pflicht und Schuldigkeit,* which plays so prominent a rôle in German literature and in German life. *Pflicht und Schuldigkeit* signifies primarily the duty and the debt which lie upon the worker to perform life's specific tasks, whatever they may be. The king in his cabinet acknowledges this obligation, the common laborer is expected to subject himself to it. No wonder that Kant, the German philosopher *par excellence,* expressed in the language of his philosophical system, in the sublime apostrophe contained in his Ethics, that supreme conception of duty as an absolute peremptory fact not to be shirked, which fits so fully the feeling of obligation as it is inherent in the German people.

It should be added, however, that the Germans are also disposed toward mystic religion. Some of the chief mystics—Meister Eckhart, Tauler, Jacob Boehme—were Germans. A recent French critic points out that the starting point of Protestantism was a mystical experience of Luther's. Goethe's poetry is deeply charged with pantheistic feeling; Wagner's music is expressive of cosmic mysticism. Now mysticism seeks to submerge the self in the all, to obliterate the sense of particularity. It therefore lies in the direction exactly opposite to the tendency toward specialization and particularization which has been dwelt upon as the main feature of German life. Mysticism may be characterized as the holiday occupation of the German soul seeking to get free of the bonds by which it is habitually tethered, to escape into wide open universal spaces and to extricate itself from the local enchainment of the task. It is a recoil against the habitual tendency. In the case of every people there are such reactions, which should be included in a complete account.

The national ideal of the English may be described as that of *noblesse oblige*. We are again, of course, attempting but a kind of shorthand sketch, a picture in the Impressionist manner. England is the dean of political liberty among the nations. She was the earliest to establish parliamentary government, and her own political institutions, and those of the self-governing colonies—that is, of the ten or twelve million whites outside of England—have come to be more and more the expression of liberal ideas. This is, of course, not true of the three hundred and fifty millions of the races subject to Britain, who are not accorded self-government, but are ruled on the principles of benevolent despotism. But in the United Kingdom itself political liberalism is firmly rooted. The suffrage has been again and again extended, until it is now almost as inclusive as in the United States. Nowhere in the world are the personal rights of the individual better protected. The Englishman is far more jealous of any infringement of his liberties than the American.

Nevertheless, the question to what extent the

AMERICAN, GERMAN AND ENGLISH IDEALS

individual shall possess rights and shall be represented in the Parliament that enacts the laws to which he is subject, is one question; and the question on what grounds he shall count among his fellows is another. There are marked inequalities of consequence and consideration in England, and here we get closer to the national ideal. How does England *rate* a man?

Once more, the system of titles, differing in England from that which is in vogue in Germany, gives us a clue. There are dukes, marquises, earls; there is plain Sir Thomas or Sir John, the baronet. And there is a constant creation of new peers and baronets. Even Mr. Bryce, the great student and eulogist of democratic commonwealths, is finally transfigured into Lord Bryce. John Morley becomes Lord Morley.

The French, on the famous night of the fourth of August, abolished their aristocracy at one stroke, a number of nobles themselves sacrificing their privileges and their titles on the altar of country. But the English, with all their progress in democratic institutions, have never abolished their nobility. Who, in sensing the national ideal, can overlook the meaning of this outstanding fact, its tribute to the ideal of the *noblesse?* Here is a *noblesse* in the traditional sense, an ancient hereditary aristocracy as the nucleus, and around it, in far greater numbers, crystallized as about a core, a modern *noblesse* of distinction in statesmanship or statecraft, in war, in commerce, also in literature, science and art—Lord Kelvin, Lord Tennyson, Lord Leighton—and this *noblesse* is looked up to as the culmination of English society, permeating all the people downward with its influence, and still possessing considerable power in the political sphere.

It is as though the English were to say: "In the constitution of every human society there must be an irrational element; pure rationality is not feasible in human affairs, it exists only in the dreams of visionaries. Now grant us as our irrational element a small number of persons counted as of the highest rank from the mere accident of birth, without regard to their merit, and let us use this irrational element as a magnet in order to gather around it a real aristocracy of distinction in all the walks of life." The English nobility has been distinguished from that of the continent by the free passage it has kept open downward among the people and upward from the people; downward because the title, whatever it be, is vested only in a single heir; the younger sons of peers being thrust down among the commoners; and upward because the ranks of the nobility are open, or at least association with the nobility is open, to men of power from whatever class. John Burns, the leader of the London dock strike, became a cabinet minister, and if he had stayed long enough might have ended by becoming Lord Burns.

The English idea, therefore, would seem to represent, subject to the inhibitions of political liberalism, the social predominance and, to a large extent, the political influence of the masterful men, of men who have gained the ascendant, each in his own class, of those who in the competitive struggle have risen to the top. The wealthy brewer may be among the number, the successful merchant, Ramsay MacDonald, perhaps, the powerful laborite. England is in this sense governed from the top, governed from above downward, however controlled by the mass.

The reason why titles do not extend in England as they do in Germany all the way through, but stop at the middle class, is now apparent. In Germany efficiency is the standard by which personal consideration is measured, and any man may be efficient in the performance of his task. In England, mastery, ascendancy is the test, and all those who have distinctly gained the ascendancy are decorated with titles and congregated at the top. But those who are below are not therefore despised. Their personal rights are safe. Their rights as electors are undisputed, their right to control and check every action of their leaders; but in point of social consequence, of value as individuals apart from rights, they are the ones who, if they have not failed in the struggle, at least have not conspicuously succeeded.

The temper of this democratized English nobility—I refer to the more recent developments, and not to ancient times—is on the whole generous. The art of government is treated as a fine art. Men of large landed property or of independent wealth set the pace, and infuse their spirit into the ruling class. The watchword is, not government by the people, but government for the people, and in England and the colonies, subject to the control of the people, government in a large, disinterested fashion.[1]

---

[1] The education of the sons of gentlemen is of a kind to produce this attitude. If Macaulay laid it down that the

AMERICAN, GERMAN AND ENGLISH IDEALS

In turning now to the national ideal of America, we discover that this defines the value of a man to consist, not in what he has achieved, nor in his ability to rise above others, but simply in his quality as a human being. America tends to appraise personality, not by what has appeared on the surface of a man's life, not by the apparent, but by the unapparent, not by the actualization, but by the spiritual possibilities, and in respect to the area of possibilities all human beings are alike.

The American ideal is that of the uncommon quality latent in the common man. Necessarily it is an ethical ideal, a spiritual ideal; otherwise it would be nonsense. For, taking men as they are, they are assuredly not equal. The differences between them, on the contrary, are glaring. The common man is not uncommonly fine spiritually, but rather, seen from the outside, "uncommonly" common. It is therefore an ethical instinct that has turned the people toward this ethical conception.

It is true that in Germany and in England,

Indian Civil Service examinations should be based on the study of the classics and mathematics, if Cecil Rhodes founded his Oxford Scholarships, it was because the classics and mathematics are not directed toward utilitarian aims, but are disinterested, and tend to encourage the disinterested point of view.

side by side with the efficiency and the mastery ideals, there has always existed this same spiritual or religious ideal; side by side with the stratification and entitulation of men, the labeling of them as lower and higher, as empirically better or worse, there has always been the recognition that men are equal—equal, that is to say, in church, but not outside, equal in the hereafter but not in this life. If we would fathom the real depth and inner significance of the democratic ideal as it slumbers or dreams in the heart of America, rather than as yet explicit, we must say that it is an ideal which seeks to overcome this very dualism, seeks to take the spiritual conception of human equality out of the church and put it into the market place, to take it from far off celestial realms for realization upon this earth. For men are not equal in the empirical sense; they are equal only in the spiritual sense, equal only in the sense that the margin of achievement of which any person is capable, be it wide or narrow, is infinitesimal compared with his infinite spiritual possibilities.

It is because of this subconscious ethical motive that there is this generous air of expectation in America, that we are always won-

AMERICAN, GERMAN AND ENGLISH IDEALS

dering what will happen next, or who will happen next. Will another Emerson come along? Will another Lincoln come along? We do not know. But this we know, that the greatest lusters of our past already tend to fade in our memory, not because we are irreverent, but because nothing that the past has accomplished can content us; because we are looking for greatness beyond greatness, truth beyond truth ever yet spoken. The Germans have a legend that in their hour of need an ancient emperor will arise out of the tomb where he slumbers to stretch his protecting hand over the Fatherland. We Americans, too, have the belief that if ever such an hour comes for us there will arise spirits clothed in human flesh amongst us sufficient for our need, but spirits that will come, as it were, out of the future to meet our advancing host and lead it, not ghosts out of the storied past. For America differs from all other nations in that it derives its inspiration from the future. Every other people has some culture, some civilization, handed down from the past, of which it is the custodian, and which it seeks further to develop. The American people have no such single tradition. They are dedicated, not to the preservation of what has been, but to the creation of what never has been. They are the prophets of the future, not the priests of the past.

I have spoken above of ideals, of what is fine in a nation, of fine tendencies. The idea which a people has of itself, like the idea which an individual has of himself, often does not tally with the reality. If we look at the realities of American life—and, on the principle of *corruptio optimi pessima,* we should be prepared for what we see—we are dismayed to observe in actual practice what seems like a monstrous caricature; not democracy, but plutocracy, kings expelled and the petty political bosses in their stead, merciless exploitation of the economically weak—a precipitate reduction of wages, for instance, at the first signs of approaching depression, in advance of what is required—instead of respect for the sacred personality of human beings the utmost disrespect. Certainly the nation needs strong and persistent ethical teaching in order to make it aware of its better self and of what is implied in the political institutions which it has founded.

But ethical teaching alone will not suffice. It must be admitted that a danger lurks in the idea of equality itself. The danger is that

AMERICAN, GERMAN AND ENGLISH IDEALS

differences in refinement, in culture, in intellectual ability and attainments are apt to be insufficiently emphasized, that the untutored, the uncultivated, the intellectually undeveloped, are apt presumptuously to put themselves on a par with those of superior development; and hence that superiority, failing to meet with recognition, will be discouraged and democracy tend to level men downward instead of upward. This will not be true so much of such moral excellence as appears in an Emerson or a Lincoln, for there is that in the lowliest which responds to the manifestations of transcendent moral beauty, but it will hold good of those minor superiorities that fall short of the highest in art and science and conduct, yet upon the fostering of which depends the eventual appearance of culture's richest fruits.

In order to ward off this danger we must have a new and larger educational policy in our schools than has yet been put in practice. Vocational training in its broadest and deepest sense will be our greatest aid.

Democracy, the American democracy, is the St. Christopher. St. Christopher bore the Christ child on his shoulders as he stepped into the river, and the child was as light as a feather,

THE WORLD CRISIS AND ITS MEANING

But it became heavier and heavier as he entered the stream, until he was well nigh borne down by it. So we, in the heyday of 1776, stepped into the stream with the infant Democracy on our shoulders, and it was light as a feather's weight; but it is becoming heavier and heavier the deeper we are getting into the stream—heavier and heavier. When we began there were four or five millions. Now there are ninety millions. Heavier and heavier! And there are other millions coming. When we began we were a homogeneous people, now there are those twenty-three languages spoken in a single school. And with this vast multitude, and this heterogeneous population, we are trying the most difficult experiment that has ever been attempted in the world, trying to invest with sovereignty the common man. There has been the sovereignty of kings, and now and then a king has done well. There has been the sovereignty of aristocracies, and now and then an English aristocracy or a Venetian aristocracy has done well—though never wholly well. And now we are imposing this most difficult task of government, which depends on the recognition of excellence in others, so that the best may rule in our behalf, on the shoulders of the multitude.

AMERICAN, GERMAN AND ENGLISH IDEALS

These are our difficulties. But our difficulties are also our opportunities. This land is the Promised Land. It is that not only in the sense in which the word is commonly taken—that is to say, a haven for the disadvantaged of other countries, a land whither the oppressed may come to repair their fortunes and breathe freely and achieve material independence. That is but one side of the promise. In that sense the Anglo-American native population is the host, extending hospitality, the benefactor of the immigrants. But this is also the land of promise for the native population themselves in order that they may be penetrated by the influence of what is best in the newcomers, in order that their too narrow horizon may be widened, in order that their stiffened mental bent may become more flexible; that festivity, pageant and song may be added to their life by the newcomers; that echoes of ancient prophecy may inspire the matter-of-fact, progressive movements, so-called, of our day.

America is the Wonderland, hid for ages in the secret of the sea, then revealed. At first, how abused! Spanish conquerors trampled it, it was the nesting place of buccaneers, adventurers, if also the home of the Puritans—bad men and good men side by side. Then for dreary centuries the home of slavery. Then the scene of prolonged strife. And now, on the surface, the stamping ground of vulgar plutocrats! And yet, in the hearts of the elect—yes, and in the hearts of the masses, too—inarticulate and dim, there has ever been present a fairer and nobler ideal, the ideal of a Republic built on the uncommon fineness in the common man! To live for that ideal is the true Americanism, the larger patriotism. To that ideal not on the field of battle, as in Europe, but in the arduous toil of peace let us be willing to give the "last full measure of devotion."

IV

THE ILLUSION AND THE IDEAL OF INTERNATIONAL PEACE

THE ideal of international peace is one of the noblest of human ideals. We cannot let ourselves think that it is illusory, destined never to be realized. On the contrary, it imperatively demands our persistent loyalty and service. But the ideal of peace is itself often envisaged in a way that turns it into an illusion. We must learn to distinguish sharply between the illusion of international peace and the true ideal.

It is roundly asserted by many at the present moment that mankind is even now learning from each day's bitter experience the lesson that war is unprofitable and barbaric, and that at the end of this present hideous struggle there will be some definitive settlement, some reorganization of society that shall exclude the future possibility of such a war. I see no reason to justify any such positive conviction. There

THE WORLD CRISIS AND ITS MEANING

are signs and evidences, it is true, of deep moral recoil against war among those who are onlookers and not participators. Our newspapers express this recoil. The war ought not to have been; nobody knows how it happened, so contrary is it to the nature of things that it did happen; and now that it has happened, surely it is for the last time. That is the strain of the discussion. But there is also a strong current running in the opposite direction, even in America—an appeal for more armaments under the plea and pretext of defense: in some cases sincerely, in other cases as a mere blind for aggressive intentions in the Far East.

Then, again, if we ask what actually is the temper among the warring peoples, those of whom it is presumed that they must be learning to hate war and preparations for war, we find that the temper of the European nations is, if possible, more militant at this time than it has ever been. For my part I have heard no complaining voices from the other side. My letters from friends abroad are filled with a more ardent spirit of belligerency than I have ever known.

In England there appeared on Christmas Day an editorial in one of the principal London

INTERNATIONAL PEACE

weeklies, *The Spectator,* concerning the war. What was the burden of this Christmas message? The editor emphasized two points, the first of which was diametrically opposed to what the pacifist editors here tell us from day to day. According to *The Spectator,* the one poignant lesson which this war should bring home is that England was not sufficiently prepared, and that she must make more complete preparation for the next war. The maxim must be reaffirmed that the only way to preserve peace is to prepare for war. England must establish compulsory military service. Every young man shall be called to the colors for four years, also serve in the first and second reserve up to fifty years of age, and so on. The other point was that the pacifists in England were chiefly to blame, not consciously, but unwittingly, for the fact that the country was unprepared. They brought on the war. They deceived Germany into believing that England would not fight. If Germany had known that England would fight she would not have entered into the war. The pacifists unconsciously and undesignedly deceived her into the belief that they could hold back England so that she would not fight. And then, when the hour of decision arrived, these very pacifists became as bellicose as the rest. It is this, says the editor, that accounts for the bitterness with which the Germans hate the English. They were crying, "Peace, Peace, Peace!" and now suddenly these same lovers of peace become most ardent fighters; surely they must be fiendish hypocrites! The lesson, therefore, the Christmas message, is—more preparation for war at the end of this war, and no more pacifist nonsense, if you please! Here, then, is a journal which represents an important section of English public opinion—and it manifests no recoil.

In Germany, as everyone knows, militancy is to-day at its culmination. This is "der heilige Krieg"; it is a holy war. In one of the German weeklies there recently appeared a poem entitled "The Four Elements." The earth is praised because it gives the opportunity for trenches; the water is praised because it gives the opportunity for submarines; fire is praised because it belches from howitzers, and the air is praised because from it explosives can be dropped!

It is also, I think, a mistake to suppose that the French people are peace-lovers. The spirit of militancy in France has never been suppressed. The French have always been a people devoted to *"La Gloire,"* and *"La Gloire"* is military glory. After the war of 1870 Jules Ferry directed the attention of his compatriots to the possible revival of Napoleon's dream of a French empire in the East. Jules Ferry's colonial adventures were, as we know, patronized by Bismarck, who desired to deflect French ambitions from Europe to the East. The military spirit has broken out in France whenever it had occasion; at the time of the Boulanger agitation, when it was supposed that Boulanger had defied Germany, and this gave him great credit; or, again, at the reception of Marchand on his return from Africa. If we may believe recent essayists, there has been more recently a decided exacerbation and aggravation of the military spirit among the younger generation— a great change, especially since the Tangier incident.

Where is the evidence of a recoil against war among the nations now engaged in warfare? How are they learning the lesson of international peace?

In turning to consider the point of difference between illusion and ideal, let us note that an

THE WORLD CRISIS AND ITS MEANING

ideal is an idea or mental picture of something that ought to be. The ideal condemns the actual. There would be no need of an ideal if the actual were what it ought to be—perfect as it ought to be. Every ideal condemns the actual, but it also as an ideal appreciates the actual in so far as the actual conditions lend themselves to betterment. There could be no ideal if the actual were not capable of being made what it ought to be. The ideal has just these two implications—always against the actual, depreciating it, and always for it, appreciating it. Now an illusion is the notion that what ought to be can be realized immediately, without working over the actual, without effort, without pain—at least with a minimum of effort and pain. We need but to form a few peace societies, build a Peace Temple at The Hague, call mass meetings and pass resolutions, recommend apparently simple devices like an international police—anything ready to hand, anything easy, to bring about what ought to be. That is characteristic of the illusion. The ideal is stern; it contemplates the actual and sees how difficult it is to change it, although it is anything but despondent, and sees that the actual certainly is capable of being changed.

INTERNATIONAL PEACE

The illusion—the immediate illusion—is that at the end of this war people will have become so tired of massacre and destruction of property that some small device, calling for but slight effort, will serve to effect the longed-for change in human society. This is the illusion which must be denounced, for it is a deception of oneself; and it is due, in a certain sense, to a moral fault in those who are obsessed by it. The illusionists are at bottom joy-loving people, who do not realize that the world is not made for enjoyment, and shirk the toil which is laid upon mankind.

It is said that the character of certain kinds of material, wood or stone, because of the grain, or one or another resistance, makes it difficult for the sculptor to work in them and to realize his ideal image. But in these resistances the true artist finds his education. He is compelled by these very obstacles in the material to ponder and consider, to mature his ideal image, to gain a closer grip of it. The difficulties which mankind experiences in moralizing the human race are like those which the artist experiences in carving the hard wood or the stone; the very difficulties are the means of educating mankind, of helping the world to visualize its ideals, to conceive them more truly, to test them, so that if they do not work perhaps because they are themselves not yet right or just, they can be further perfected. The resistance we meet is a challenge compelling us to mature our moral ideals, and the justification of our efforts in the world lies precisely in the closer grip we obtain on ideal realities. It is never in the fact that we house them in the actual world. That we never do. Our reward is in our surer understanding, our firmer possession of the ideal as reality.

It sometimes happens that an illusion is due to pity. Under very great stress, deep feeling is apt to breed illusions. For instance, you see the suffering of the poor. The more your pity is stirred up the less are you willing to wait for a remedy. This state of things, you exclaim, is intolerable, and there must be relief. Therefore you ask for a cure that will work at once. But the real remedies never work in that way. They work slowly, gradually. Yet, when feeling is wrought up, then a gradual remedy is scouted; you insist on one that shall work promptly and completely. That is the origin of social Utopias.

Such also is the origin of the illusion of

peace. Our feelings are wrought up; we hear about the massacres; the young men, the flower of Europe, are being slain; mothers are deprived of their sons, sweethearts of their lovers, wives of their husbands. We say: this is intolerable, we cannot endure it; we cry out for a remedy, a quick remedy, for something that promises to give immediate relief.

Now the danger is that people whose feelings are very much wrought up will overlook the real difficulties in the way of removing the evil condition. The illusionist often does more harm than good. It may be that he does good in stirring up our conscience. But he also paves the way for disappointment, disillusion. Those who indulge in the hope of a quick and a durable peace are apt to single out such factors in the actual situation as seem favorable to their dream, but ignore or are incapable of estimating those that are opposed to their remedy. They fasten on international courts, as if the case of strife between nations were the same as that between individuals. Or they depend on pity, and say pity will conquer; sympathy has more power and is more general to-day than ever before. Or why cannot we appeal to self-interest? War is unprofitable to the victor and the vanquished, said Jean Bloch and Norman Angell—and war, utterly unprofitable war, presently happened. There are certain factors in the situation which give a plausible color to the quick remedies, while the illusionists overlook the things that make for war.

Let us direct our attention for a moment to certain of the more permanent conditions that make for war. One would not wish to dampen the belief in peace, but rather to dispel the illusion—as if the Golden Vision were entering the gate, as if the beautiful feet of those who bring glad tidings of peace were already discernible on the mountains. The habit of seeing things as they are is indispensable to moral earnestness. It is immoral not to try to see things as they are. We can only overcome difficulties if we first clearly see them.

There are certain causes of the war which have not been sufficiently noticed. One of them is the world unrest. We speak of social unrest, but there is also a world unrest. Egypt is stirred up. Stationary China is all aroused. India is restless. The Mohammedan world is disturbed. There is a great unrest the world over. No one knows exactly what has caused it. There sometimes seem to be quasi-meteoric

INTERNATIONAL PEACE

changes that affect the psychic atmosphere. The celebrated historian, von Ranke, called attention to the fact that at the very time when the Protestant Reformation broke out in Europe there were reformatory movements that had no connection with Luther's movement in other parts of the globe. Furthermore, peoples, just like individuals, have the instinct of self-preservation. Now the fact is that the internal conditions of the peoples who are at war to-day were all more or less disturbed. England was on the verge of civil war. The Irish Nationalists and the Ulsterites had come almost to open strife. Von Buelow, only a year before the outbreak, characterized the social democracy of Germany as the unforgivable enemy, against whom it must be war to the knife. The condition of Russia is that of chronic simmering revolution. In France the instability of conditions was illustrated by the infamous Caillaux trial, that came to a close on the very day before the outbreak of the war. France was rent by internal divisions, the Clericals opposing the Radicals, monarchists without an adequate pretender chafing under the republican constitution, the Republicans themselves split up into numerous groups, Socialists with a program which they never came approximately near to carrying out—the whole situation impossible. Then came war with Germany, and immediately the strife was hushed and the nation gathered itself together into a unity, all its warring members harmonized by joint action against the foe.

Another cause of profound trouble in Europe is that Europe is like an apartment house, crowded with many families, living at too close quarters, speaking different languages, and in each other's way. America is like one of our old New England villages, every house having its own lawn and garden and standing off comfortably from its neighbors. In Europe you cannot travel twelve hours without crossing different frontiers, meeting people of extremely different types, who speak different languages and have different historical traditions. We forget this when we offer the American type as a pattern on which the reorganization of Europe should be planned. People speak of the United States of Europe, but it is forgotten that a federal government can only be successful if the same type of government is represented in all the component members. In America we have one and the same type of govern-

INTERNATIONAL PEACE

ment in Washington and in all the forty-eight States. In fact, the Constitution commands that the federal power shall guarantee a republican form of government to each of the States. But Europe includes an autocracy pure and simple in Russia, a modified autocracy in Germany (modified by the Reichstag), a parliamentary cabinet government in England, a centralized democracy in France—unlike ours because it is centralized. You have two principles combined in France. However republican its legislation, the administration is still that which was transmitted by Napoleon; it is centralized, monarchical. Each of these European States has its own type of government. How, then, can there be a United States of Europe? The suggestion has been made that the United States of Europe should be republican; that would mean superimposing a republican form of government upon nations not one of which has yet attained in its own affairs to the republican type.

Another difficulty lies in the difference in the stage of civilization reached. One often hears the remark that Russia is the weak spot in the moral case of the Allies. But Russia is bound to be a very important factor in the European

THE WORLD CRISIS AND ITS MEANING

situation in the future. Numerically Russia is the most powerful of the European nations. And the fact that Russia is an autocracy, with eighty per cent of her population not able to read or write, is not only a weak spot in the case of the Allies, but a tremendously perilous spot in the future of European civilization.

A last point to be noted in this connection, as explaining the new militant spirit, is the fact that religion has largely died out among the intellectual class. Now, religion having been lost, and the need of some ideal still being felt, patriotism has come to take its place. Men tire, after all, of self-interest. There is nothing so wearisome as self-seeking, and a world devoid of religious belief is turning to the ideal of country as something great, something worth sacrificing for. It is for this reason that the Germans speak of the war as "der heilige Krieg." There is something holy in getting away from one's miserable self. There are dignity and luster, there is something grand and exalting in devotion to one's land. It is the disappearance of religion that accounts to no small degree for this exaltation of patriotism.

The ideal both condemns the actual and ap-

INTERNATIONAL PEACE

preciates it. It sees in actual life the possibility of betterment, of things coming to be in time as they ought to be. Now what are the forces upon which we shall rely for help in the actualization of the ideal of peace? Whether they work slowly or quickly is not the question, so that they do not lead to disappointing reactions, as the illusions do. What are the forces actually existent in the world upon which we can count to check and overcome those antagonistic forces to which I have referred above?

And here we get a flash of illumination from that idyll in the New Testament in which is related the story of the birth of Jesus. The shepherds watched their flocks by night and the heavens opened and the angels sang "Gloria in excelsis Deo!"—Glory to God in the highest, and on earth peace to men of His good will. That is to say, the men who have that divine good will shall have peace. According to this rendering, the song of the angels did not announce that peace should be bestowed upon all men indiscriminately—that presently there should be universal peace among men—but peace conditionally *to men who have the good will*. This is my point, that good will in the strict sense is the engine upon which we must

THE WORLD CRISIS AND ITS MEANING

rely to create peace. In the first place, every one of us, instead of writing letters to the newspaper as to what the Kaiser or the Czar or someone else should do, may begin to initiate the reign of peace by creating in himself good will, especially towards the people against whom he feels objection. Some object to colored people, some to Jews, some to Poles, some to the Japanese. Almost everyone objects to one or more other races, and many people object to all races other than their own. There are also individuals that repel us, there are those whose mere faces create in us dislike. We can begin by overcoming our personal repulsions, making it our ethical purpose, if we feel strongly repelled, to try and take a friendly view of a man, to try and see the fair side of his nature. Like St. Francis in the legend, bathe your lepers, tend those who are repugnant to you. If there is anyone whom you particularly dislike, think kindly of him at this moment. He is your leper—see whether you cannot imitate St. Francis and be in thought and deed his friend.

A second means of engendering good will towards Frenchmen and Germans and Russians and Englishmen is to learn to appreciate their contributions to civilization. We are often pitifully ignorant of the finer qualities both of the European and the Oriental nations. Just as we teach biology in the schools, and the natural history of animals, we should teach also about the different types of human beings. Why should we not have a science of nations as we have a science of biology? Familiarity will breed respect. Good will towards other people depends upon our knowing more about them than we do, and a brief, compendious course on the Science of Nations should be included in the curriculum of high schools and colleges. An attempt in this direction was made in one of our universities during the past winter, and with good success.

Two other practical devices are being constantly urged, which should be considered from the point of view of the proposition laid down above, that good will is the only possible foundation of permanent peace. The first, that of an international court, implies reliance on the impartial decisions of judges to compose the feuds of nations. Do the impartial decisions of judges serve to create good will? To a certain extent they do. A judge stands between the party that would violate rights and the party whose rights are being infringed upon.

THE WORLD CRISIS AND ITS MEANING

Men in the long run learn to respect the rights which they cannot with impunity disregard. But this is only after many sharp lessons have been taught; and the respect thus learned, unless other deeper influences are present to assist, is a precarious, external respect. The history of litigation amply bears out this statement. To take a practical instance, let us suppose that Germany and France were to go before the Hague Tribunal and leave it to the judges to decide whether Alsace and Lorraine should continue to be embodied with the one or restored to the other, both parties agreeing to submit, and actually submitting to the verdict. Would the people against whom the decision had been rendered be filled with increasing good will, which is the foundation of enduring peace, toward the other? Is it not more than likely that they would be animated with a more intensified grudge?

In a previous chapter I have touched upon the insuperable difficulty of securing impartial judges, in view of the small number of nations, and also the difficulty of securing observance of their decisions by the proposed employment of an international police—a doubtful expedient, since the police would need to be in fact large

INTERNATIONAL PEACE

enough and sufficiently well equipped to overcome the armed forces of a recalcitrant nation, thus becoming in effect itself an army and ceasing to be a police.

But there is another difficulty which must be faced. The conception of the Hague Court as it exists in the public mind is vitiated by a radical ambiguity as to function. It is sometimes conceived as an arbitration tribunal, and in that case it lacks the essential features of an arbitrating body, it being peremptory that such a body shall include an adequate representation of the parties in dispute, with an umpire in addition. The Hague Tribunal, consisting for the most part of lawyers and men who have seen diplomatic service, does not provide for adequate representation of the parties in dispute. Again, the Hague Tribunal is sometimes also conceived, as in Mr. Knox's proposal of an international Prize Court, as a true court, and in that case the fatal objection to it is that, like all such juristic bodies, it will inevitably tend to base its findings on precedent, whereas in the dissensions between nations new situations are constantly arising which cannot be settled on the basis of precedent, but only by a vital apprehension of the facts at issue. Hence

THE WORLD CRISIS AND ITS MEANING

in the discussion of this matter the cry has constantly been raised, and not by the ignoble-minded only, that vital interests shall not be submitted to a court of judges sitting in their cool, remote sanctuary at The Hague. And yet it is just the differences with respect to vital interests that lead to tension and to final rupture. If these are excluded, then the Hague Tribunal must be remitted to a secondary place among the instruments of international amity. In that place only will it serve a useful purpose. In any event, it does not naturally engender that prime requisite, good will.

The second proposal, frequently urged, is that secret diplomacy should be abolished, and the parliaments, or the nations directly, by referendum or plebiscite, shall be called upon to say Yea or Nay whenever a war is in prospect. The obvious objection is that a great multitude, especially when it becomes tumultuous under the influence of excitement, is even more rash and headlong in its resolves than a government. At the time of the Spanish-American war it was public opinion that overbore Congress, and it was the pressure coming from Congress that forced the hand of the administration. President McKinley and Speaker Reed did their utmost to hold back the torrent, but in vain.

But from the point of view here taken there is another and more vital objection. The motive relied upon by the advocates of the referendum is that of self-interest. It is believed that the men who would be called to the colors, who would have to leave their families, foreseeing possible widowhood for their wives and orphanhood for their children, the citizens who would have to pay the war taxes, would hesitate before they accepted these burdens; in a word, that those who would have to suffer the losses entailed by war would be slow to engage in it unless under most urgent and irresistible provocation. But the facts prove the contrary. In the frenzy of a contagious passion that seizes the masses, consideration is thrown to the winds, and the checks of reason snap like dry twigs. And even if it were not so, if the self-regarding motives were more coercive than they are, they would still not guarantee that attitude of good will towards other peoples which, as we hold, is essential to the foundation of peace. Such good will is the will to acknowledge the justice of the claims of one's opponents in so far as they are just. It is the will to be fair towards one's adversaries, and, in order to be fair, the will to see the matter in dispute through the eyes of one's opponents. For such fairness neither the popular referendum nor the vote on war by each parliament sitting separately, makes provision. Congress in Washington or the parliament in London or in Paris would still be looking at the matter through their own eyes. In each parliament the members would be corroborating each other in their one-sided view. The essence of fairness, that of putting oneself in another's place, seeing through another's eyes, would not be achieved. If, indeed, all of the parliaments of the nations about to go to war could be assembled together, if the representatives of one people could be confronted with those of the other people, man to man, if each could get to see the other's side, not through the distorted medium of diplomatic dispatches or colored reports, but by looking into each other's faces, hearing the accents of each other's voices, the case would be different. Now in this form the plan of confrontation may not be possible. But in another form it seems possible, and this leads to the third suggestion which I should like to submit.

To avert war let there be an international

INTERNATIONAL PEACE

conference or congress assembled, not consisting merely of diplomats, of governments and their agents only, as would have been the proposed conference at London, which Germany declined to attend, but a conference or congress consisting of representatives of the laboring class, of the manufacturing class, of the chambers of commerce, of the agriculturists, of the universities, of each country—say two for each of the groups mentioned within each nation. This would not make a numerically unmanageable assembly. Let there be strict rules adopted, providing that each side and each of the groups represented on each shall be heard without interruption. I venture to say that if Liebknecht and Sudekum, Jaurès and Guesde, had faced each other in such a conference; if the British merchants who, only a year or two before the outbreak of the war, paid friendly visits to the merchants of Düsseldorf, had met their German hosts at such a conference, the bloody issue might have been avoided and a means of compromise discovered. The difficulties, everyone realizes, are enormous: not questions on the surface, but the deep tendencies of which these questions are but the external symptom, constitute the difficulties. Great

Britain holds and intends to maintain as long as her fingers are not too nerveless to grasp it, the trident of the seas. There is much to be said in her favor, seeing that she depends for her food supply on the waterways. But why supremacy? There is much to be said on the other side on behalf of upward striving commercial peoples whose prospects likewise depend upon the freedom of the waterways. Germany desires territorial expansion; there is much to be said for that. But as to the methods used there is not a little to be said on the other side. Impelled by pan-Slavism, Russia desires to embrace within her dominion the southern Slavs now included in the Austrian Empire. Austria resists disintegration. The difficulties, as soon as the actual concrete questions involved receive attention, are seen to be intricate, and yet not therefore insuperable. Compromise is the solution of similar clashes of interest within the political circumscription of each nation; compromise must be the solution in respect to the opposition of interests in the international domain—but compromise based, since there can be no superordinated sovereignty overarching the nations of Europe, on the spirit of fairness and good will, on the will to see the matter in

INTERNATIONAL PEACE

controversy from the point of view of the opponent as well as from one's own.

When not only the governments through their agents meet, but the people meet through their representatives, the labor delegates, the merchant delegates, the delegates of the peasantry, and the rest, then should be exemplified what appears to me a psychological truth, namely, that justice, fairness, respect for rights, are produced when we see and hear the very person who claims to have those rights in the uprising of his manhood assert them, expound them, plead for them. It is under such circumstances that rights cease to be abstractions; it is then that the personality which possesses the rights, or claims to possess them, compels us to give heed. We can flout and trample on the rights of others so long as we hear of them only at a distance, or so long as those we infringe upon can be kept mute; but we cannot hear justice uttered and not be shaken, and at least in part succumb. It is for this reason that employers who have not the good will and do not desire to be fair, refuse to receive delegations of their employees. It is for this reason that the landlord class in England and the *bourgeoisie* under Louis Philippe in France refused representation to the artisan and laboring class in parliament. They did not intend to grant them their human rights, and therefore they did well to prevent the voice, the irresistible voice, of Justice from being heard. If you wish to do wrong to any individual or to any class or to any people, stop their mouths, or stop your ears, or shout so loud that their voice may be drowned. And this is precisely what the nations of Europe are doing, every one of them—shouting so loud in the press and in their manifestoes that the voice of the other side, and the quotum of justice on the other side, may not produce its effect. It is on this psychological truth that I base the suggestion that there shall be international congresses, not of diplomats as heretofore, but of the people through their chosen representatives, so that each people may be compelled to face and hear the people or peoples that are its opponents.

This is a wholly different proposal from that of a European parliament, superior to all minor parliaments. Such a plan is assuredly Utopian; but an international congress called together for a particular purpose may serve to meet another great need which, so far as I have learned, is commonly ignored in the discussion—namely,

INTERNATIONAL PEACE

the need of some kind of an international legislature. We are constantly being referred to the Court at The Hague as the instrument for settling disputes. But while a court is the proper organ for administering law, a legislative body is the proper instrument for creating law. The distinction between the legislative, the judicial and the executive powers is one of the great achievements of modern political experience. Are we to ignore this in the international field? Here, too, there must be, side by side with the judiciary, an international legislature, a congress consisting of the same elements as already enumerated, meeting from time to time for the express purpose of creating and developing the law which the court is to interpret. And there is the greatest need of developing international law. Every student of the subject admits that what is called international law is in many respects beneath the demands of the better conscience of our time. Consider only that the brute right of conquest is still untouched in international law, or touched only in the most timorous and tentative fashion; that it is not yet prohibited by international law for the conqueror to impose a crushing indemnity on the conquered, irrespective of the rightfulness or wrongfulness of the war in the first instance; that the conqueror is not prohibited by international law from annexing conquered territory, and annexing the people that live on it as though they were so many cattle. A law-making body we need, as well as an international court, and it is the people, and not the lawyers and the diplomats alone, from whom legislation should emanate.

Till now we have had two alternatives: the foreign affairs of nations managed largely in the dark by governments and their diplomatic servants, by executives who find it easy to create situations in which the people have no choice except to follow where their rulers may lead them; and now we have the proposal that each people alone in its parliament should decide. But this also is no solution; on the contrary, it is putting a premium on precipitate and passionate action, and offers no guarantees of fairness. An international law-making body, consisting of representatives of the peoples, would seem to be the wiser measure.

If, then, there be any who believe that when this war ends the Golden Age will set in, if not of universal blessedness, at least of universal agreement to abstain forever after from the

INTERNATIONAL PEACE

use of weapons, this is surely the illusion of peace. The ideal of peace involves rather the active and unremitting effort to employ those psychic and moral forces in human nature which make for the development of international good will.

More than two thousand years ago Isaiah, or some writer who used his name, foretold in an ecstasy of moral enthusiasm that the time would come when two things should happen: the ferocities inherent in the wild things of the forest would be turned into gentleness, the predatory nature of the wolf would be changed, he would dwell with the lamb. And secondly, men would beat their swords into plowshares and their spears into pruning hooks, and no one any longer would learn the art of war. And both things were to happen by miraculous intervention from on high.

The cruel, anti-moral forces in nature we cannot alter; the anti-moral instincts in human nature it is within our power to change—but not by folding our hands and waiting for a miracle. Twenty centuries have elapsed and the miracle has not been wrought; other centuries may elapse and the miracle still be unperformed. But by patient effort, by a more penetrating ethical teaching, and by the wit and wisdom to create institutions and instrumentalities suitable to foster the better traits, we may work for, if we shall not live to see, the time when the angelic song shall be fulfilled, of peace among men because they shall have learned to take towards one another the essential inward attitude of good will.

V

CIVILIZATION AND PROGRESS IN THE LIGHT OF THE PRESENT WAR

IT is, above all, important to distinguish between civilization and morality. The two are commonly confused. In the interest of clearness it is indispensable that they be kept apart.

What do we mean by civilization? Babylon had a civilization of its own; so did Thebes, so did Carthage, Rome. On what principle shall we discriminate between the different types of civilization—assigning higher value to some than to others? And how discriminate between a civilized state of society and a condition of things ethically satisfactory? The ethical condition of society, that in which society shall achieve ethical perfection, is the ideal end. Civilization is *only* a means to that end. To prefer the means civilization to the end moral perfection, as the miser prefers gold to its uses, is a fatal error, and it is the underlying

THE WORLD CRISIS AND ITS MEANING

cause that has brought on this worldwide war. On the other hand, one is bound to remember that civilization, if only a means, is indispensable to the end; and the different kinds of civilization are to be rated as high or low in proportion as they are more or less conducive to the ultimate goal towards which humanity's face is set.

But a more explicit definition is required. Civilization then, let us say, is the sum total of the instrumentalities that sustain and promote the higher interests of man, such as science, art, religion, and, embracing them all, ethical perfection.

For instance, language is a necessary instrument of rational existence. A community is the more civilized the richer and the more flexible the language it uses, the more capable of receiving the imprint of complex patterns of thinking, and of transmitting subtle shades of feeling. The civilized Greeks were set off against the barbarians by the exquisite adaptation of their language to the uses of the imagination and the intellect.

Great libraries, as in ancient Babylon and Alexandria, and to-day in all the capital cities of the world, are constituents of civilization,

CIVILIZATION AND THE WAR

promoting as they do the progress of knowledge. Schools, colleges, universities, with their laboratories, belong in the same class.

Temples like the Parthenon, cathedrals, churches, synagogues and mosques, with their solemn rituals, are elements of civilization on the religious side.

Law courts and the systems of jurisprudence they administer, are capital factors in civilization.

The manners of a people, rude and harsh or polished and informed by courtesy, are an index of the degree of civilization to which they have attained.

Commerce and industry, in particular, loom large in the current conceptions of civilization —too large if the thoughts to be presented in this chapter are correct. In reading some of the recent works on the subject, one might almost suppose that the progress of man, during all the millenniums that have elapsed since his emergence out of the lowest depths of savagery, has been tending toward the modern system of trade and manufacture as to its apogee. There is a school of writers who arrange the entire history of the race in periods according to the technical invention characteristic of each

—such as the use of fire, the ceramic art, the smelting of iron, the invention of gunpowder and of the printing press—the whole series culminating in the steam engine, and what has followed since. This is, in truth, but a partial view to take of an intricate matter, but we need not linger to discuss it. What it concerns us to remember is that civilization, whatever its vicissitudes, has never yet coincided with a condition of society which could be considered morally acceptable. And there are three obvious signs of this want of congruity.

One is that a highly civilized state of society may coexist together with internal moral decay. This is notorious. The state of Rome in the latter days of the Empire, the court of France in the days of Louis XIV and Louis XV, are commonplace examples. The reason is that civilization, or the set of instrumentalities that serve the higher purposes of life, may continue to exist without any longer being used for the higher purposes. The temples exist, but the religion that is taught in them becomes obsolete or obsolescent. The law courts are in operation, but the underlying conceptions of law no longer embody the social sense of the community. Literature is produced, but it has

CIVILIZATION AND THE WAR

lost its seriousness. The salt has lost its savor. We cannot say that Paris, in the days preceding the Revolution, had ceased to be a civilized city. Quite the contrary; but the gap between the extant civilization and the moral consciousness of the people was wide, and a gap of this kind always exists to a greater or less degree.

A second sign is that the benefits of the instrumentalities which we call civilization have in most civilized states never been at the disposal of more than a minority. In civilized communities the life of the majority is more or less uncivilized.

The third sign is the flagrant conduct of the civilized peoples toward the uncivilized. A moral person, in proportion as he is inspired by ethical motives, is moral precisely in his conduct toward the unmoral. The real goodness of a man can best be tested by his conduct toward the bad. The incongruity between civilization and morality, on the other hand, is set in striking relief by the wickedness which the civilized nations have exhibited in their behavior toward the weaker races of the globe.

It is this point that I wish to labor. I have already indicated that I believe it to be the fundamental cause of the present world strife.

THE WORLD CRISIS AND ITS MEANING

The chief European nations are at bottom engaged in mortal combat at home for the sake of dominion abroad. Though the conflict is waged on European soil, the prize lies outside of Europe, in the East. The struggle we are witnessing is a struggle for the maintenance or achievement of world dominance, or of a share in it. The apple of discord is dominion over the weaker races. Germany and England to-day are the protagonists in full view. But Russia, extending her empire over the north of Europe and Asia, trampling on Persia, seeking to envelop China, is moved by the same immense, instinctive propulsion toward domination. France under Jules Ferry revived Napoleon's dream of an Oriental empire, pushed into Tunis, and but a few years ago successfully tightened her grip on Morocco. Italy has laid hold of Cyrenaica and is stirring up within herself ancient memories of Roman sway on the shores of the Mediterranean.

The British Empire is increasing by leaps and bounds. It furnishes the most instructive example of successful imperialism, of silent and incessant territorial aggrandizement. A glance at the map of Africa as it was in 1870, and as it had been altered by 1900, exhibits the almost

CIVILIZATION AND THE WAR

avalanche-like advance of England's supremacy in the Dark Continent. During that brief period of about three recent decades, the population of the empire increased by eighty-eight millions, while the number of square miles added amounted to between four and five millions.[1]

Access to foreign markets, control of the sources of the supply of colonial products, preferential treatment in the matter of railway and mining concessions and the like, opportunities for profitable foreign investments—these are the material advantages that feed the fires of imperialism. And combined with these there is the craving for power, as displayed in ruling subject-races, in holding down vast populations.[2] Wealth and power for the West attained by overlordship in the East is the twofold aim of imperialism.

[1] During the same period Germany added sixteen millions to her population, and about one million square miles to her territorial possessions. The total population of the British Empire at present is estimated at from four hundred and twenty to four hundred and fifty millions.

[2] The fact that a mere handful of Englishmen garrisoned in the country are able to assert mastery over three hundred and fifty millions of people in India is naturally incense to the pride of the rulers. (Compare Sir Charles Dilke's remarks in "Greater Britain" on the "romance connected with our Indian possessions," and Lord Cromer's frank affirmation of the *animus manendi* in ancient and modern imperialism.)

THE WORLD CRISIS AND ITS MEANING

The war at present waged is a war of rival imperialisms. The chief European states are playing for position in Europe, for salient points there from which to strike effectively for dominion in Asia and Africa. In their push eastward their paths have crossed each other, they have come into collision, and this worldwide explosion has been the result. Austria, with Germany behind her, has been urging toward the Ægean and Asia Minor. In so doing she has threatened to block the lines of Russia's advance. The French Republic, not less imperialistic than the monarchies, came into collision with Italy in North Africa. Germany, more conspicuous at the present moment than the rest, has undertaken to dispute with England the supremacy of the seas, which is equivalent to supremacy in the East, and aims to secure for herself a place in the sun in lands of the sun.

In the current discussion of the war, the occasions have, as a rule, been taken for the causes, or the proximate causes have arrested attention to the neglect of the radical cause. The questions we have hotly debated are: Who threw the fat in the fire? Who is immediately responsible for this outbreak? Was it Austria

CIVILIZATION AND THE WAR

with her arrogant demand on Servia? Was it the Kaiser? Was Russia really mobilizing on the German frontier? Was England, as the Germans persist in believing, perfidiously taking advantage of Germany's isolation to crush her growing navy? But these questions, important as they may be, will probably not be settled with any approach to impartiality until our posterity shall take them up in cooler blood, and with a more complete knowledge of the documents and the facts involved. The point I wish to urge is that all these questions relate to the occasions and not to the ultimate cause of the strife. We are fascinated at present by those aspects of the war that obtrude themselves upon our attention, and excite our passions and our indignation. The violation of Belgian neutrality and its bloody consequences, the vast armies swaying forward and backward, the loss of so many precious lives, the untold suffering of innocent non-combatants— these things naturally and inevitably bulk large in our view, and we forget, or relegate to a secondary place, the really most vital question of all, namely, What blame ought to attach to *all* the belligerents, to those who in this immediate contest have the larger measure of

THE WORLD CRISIS AND ITS MEANING

justice on their side? and to those who have not—the question, *What is wrong in our civilization as a whole,* what deep flaw penetrates it to its core, what is the radical cause that has led to this universal strife?

A huge race is being run. The nations of the Occident are racing toward the Orient. At the starting-point in Europe there has occurred a scuffle among the racers, each pushing for position. One of them, a smaller competitor, Belgium, has been ruthlessly trampled down. The others have come to blows. We are asking who in this scuffle is right and who is wrong. Does it never occur to ask whether they are not all wrong, whether the race they are running is legitimate, whether the goal they are trying for—supremacy over the weaker races—belongs to them?

In plain words, what right have the stronger races to hold the weaker in subjection? What business has France in Morocco? What right had Germany or the others to penetrate into China? What right has England, a nation of forty millions, to rule over three hundred and fifty millions in India? What moral credentials can imperialism show for itself? As a matter of fact, as everyone knows, England

CIVILIZATION AND THE WAR

went into India for trade.[1] Now the extension of trade, the establishment of commercial relations, peacefully if possible, forcibly if necessary, seems to be fallaciously regarded as a sufficient warrant for the intrusion of stronger nations upon the land and property belonging to the weaker. Commerce and civilization are mistakenly identified. To extend or force commerce, even upon reluctant peoples, besides being profitable to the trader, is supposed to be a sort of sacred mission on behalf of civilization. But trade is only one of the factors of civilization, and the methods employed in spreading it may be and often are of such a character as to undo other and more valuable factors of civilization, and to defeat the very ends for which alone civilization is worth while.

In surveying the recent dealings of white men with colored peoples, on the Congo, in Brazil, in Peking at the time of the Boxer Revolution, we realize with something like dismay the fearful consequences to which this fatal fallacy of identifying trade and civilization has led. The abominable behavior of the white

[1] She was led by commercialism, and slipped into imperialism. It is significant that everywhere there should be this connection between the two—commercialism is the parent and imperialism the offspring.

man in his contact with men of darker skin, the crimes in which he has indulged, are sure to remain the most disgraceful blot on the nineteenth century. In a review of a recent book on Africa I find it estimated that ten millions of the natives have been killed off in consequence of the incoming of the white race, in part directly, in part by the infernal sale of spirituous liquor, in part by the communication of obscene diseases which civilized man has brought with him. In his valuable study of this subject, Mr. J. A. Hobson expresses the belief that extermination or subjugation is the fate which commercialism, in the guise of imperialism, has in store for defenseless native populations. And the facts he adduces seem to bear out his terrible contention. But if this be so, are we not putting the cart before the horse in our spreading of so-called civilization? Is the violation of human life and liberty compensated for by the material gains? Do men exist for the sake of things or not rather things for the sake of men? Are the building of railways, the stretching of telegraph lines, the increase of the stock of rubber, to be set up as ends in themselves, having a value and a sort of sacredness on their own account?

CIVILIZATION AND THE WAR

The fallacy involved may perhaps be formulated in the following proposition: The whole earth belongs to the whole of mankind. Wherever there is a piece of soil capable of yielding a rich return, wherever there are stored away under the surface deposits of coal and iron, gems or precious metals, it is to the interest of mankind as a whole, in order to enlarge the supply of the products to be exchanged among them, that this soil be made to bear its fruits, that these precious deposits be brought out of the dark to the surface. Hence it seems to follow that wherever on any territory a people subsist too backward or too indolent to win these fruits of the soil, or to bring these treasures to the light, it is right that they be dispossessed, exterminated if need be, or coerced to servile labor by more alert and active peoples that are ready to step into their places. This may be baldly stated, but it seems, so far as I am able to judge, to express the fundamental proposition on which imperialism—the so-called right of the civilized races to occupy the lands of backward peoples—depends.

But to this view of the connection between territory and population a wholly different conception is to be opposed. Humanity, mankind

THE WORLD CRISIS AND ITS MEANING

as a whole, has a vested interest primarily, not in the land and its products, be they on the earth or under the earth, but in human beings and their mental and moral development. Every people, every tribe, however little advanced in its stage of development, represents a certain psychic type or pattern. It is in the interest of humanity as such that there shall be on the globe the greatest variety of these patterns, and hence that every psychic type be preserved and assisted to its more distinct expression. The territory is related to the people that inhabit it as the body is related to the individual: it is the physical substratum indispensable to its psychic existence and growth. As little as the body may be taken from an individual, so little can the land be rightly taken from the people who have their roots in it. The people, therefore, are the primary consideration, the land the secondary and subsidiary. The interest of humanity is in the preservation and the education of peoples, and only to a lesser degree in the wealth production of the soil.

It follows from this that the more advanced peoples hold, indeed, a trust for civilization. But the condition of this trust is respect for

CIVILIZATION AND THE WAR

the independence of every people, and its fulfillment involves an educative function, designed to lead the backward peoples to a full utilization of the opportunities afforded by their environment, and to the working out of their distinctive mental character in the process of utilizing those opportunities. The function of the civilized nations is to educate the uncivilized, not to exterminate or subjugate them.

But the claim is that imperialism at its best, of which England is the fairest example, is aware of this obligation and fulfills it. Is not English rule in India an educative force? Does not England maintain order and security throughout the Peninsula, and justice as between man and man in the courts of law? And does she not thereby educate the people in the essentials of a civilized society? She keeps them from cutting each other's throats and gives them justice—and what more can be demanded? We are bound, therefore, to push our inquiry further: does she respect their independence? Does she give evidence of an intention to prepare them for self-government, to put them on their feet politically? Heirs of a great tradition in religion, philosophy and in art, they are indisputably in many respects a highly civilized people. If they are feeble politically, does England as their schoolmaster intend to develop in them the power of self-direction? The acts of the Indian Government afford no certain evidence of any such intention, while British imperialism, speaking from the lips of Lord Cromer, expressly disavows any such intention. Whatever measure of self-government, he declares, may now or hereafter be granted to the Indian people, the possibility of eventual withdrawal is to be explicitly excluded. The *animus manendi,* the deliberate will to remain the masters of the Indian people, is directly affirmed.

The critics of English rule complain of the burden of supporting the military establishment. They complain that the provisions made for education are extremely scanty—an annual appropriation of twelve million dollars for the more than three hundred million of the population in India, when the city of New York alone expends thrice that amount on her schools. They complain that the fine arts of India have been practically annihilated by the influx of inferior European commodities. They admit, as everyone must admit, the high integrity and the disinterested devotion that characterize the English administration, and they acknowledge the two invaluable benefits which England has bestowed—order, and justice in the courts of law. But they insist, these critics do, that we be thoroughgoing. They press upon us the urgent query whether justice between individuals is enough, whether it can compensate for the intrinsic injustice that is practiced toward the people as a whole by the very fact that it is intended to hold them in permanent tutelage to alien masters.

England upholds the principles of liberalism only for white men, for the one-tenth of the population of the British Empire that is included within the United Kingdom, and for the twelve million that inhabit the self-governing colonies of Canada, Australia, etc. But towards the three hundred and fifty millions of India the principle which England upholds is not that of liberalism, but of despotism—a beneficent despotism, at least since the Sepoy Mutiny, but a despotism still. These things are said by the critics,[1] and ought to be heeded,

---

[1] See also Sir Charles Dilke's frank avowal of the despotic nature of the British Government in India in his book on "The Problems of Greater Britain."

because they bring into view the present disposition to defend imperialism by insufficient moral pretexts, to stop short at the lesser justice between individual and individual, and to ignore the larger justice that is due between people and people.

We can have no better authority for this point of view than Lord Cromer himself, whose fascinating personality evokes admiration, not only because of his great ability, but of his utter freedom from cant. Lord Cromer asserts, as we have seen, the *animus manendi*, the intention to stay. Your masters we are, he tells the subject races, and your masters we intend to remain. But he does not deceive himself as to the terms on which this mastery is to be maintained. Material interests, he points out, are the bonds that tie Egypt to England; and the Indian people submit to our rule because they must, but with no affection or gratitude toward their rulers. The English have not succeeded in conciliating the good will of their multitudinous subjects. Only he adds that the French have done no better in Algiers, despite appearances, and that the Russians have done no better in Central Asia, and that the case of England is not essentially different from that of any of the other Western powers that have encroached upon the East. And he gives the reason. The reason is that the natives feel an inveterate and insurmountable repugnance to being subject to men who are aliens to them, aliens in blood, in customs, in belief. And the more the natives are educated, the more Western ideas penetrate through the medium of Western influence, the more intolerable becomes to them the alien rule under which they live.

Are they not right, these natives who resent and some day will resist the rule of aliens? Does not independence mean self-direction? And is not the right of self-direction for a people as much as for an individual a primary moral demand? Can there be justice in the world among nations as long as this primary moral demand on the part of those who are at present weaker is denied by those who are stronger? And if all the belligerents in the present war have acted in Asia and Africa on the principle that might makes right—can we wonder that the same principle should be proclaimed in Europe? Can the strong act unjustly toward the weak and not fall out among themselves? This is an aspect of the world situation to-day that is too much overlooked; it seems to be the most fundamentally important of all.

Under these circumstances, how futile is it merely to decry militarism as the cause of all this evil, and to represent the crushing of militarism as the remedy! Militarism is but the tool. Militarism, if you please, is the gun, but "the man behind the gun" is commercialism, industrialism, imperialism—in fine, the spirit of aggression, by whatever name it may be called. So long as this spirit of aggression remains unchecked, so long as strong peoples permit themselves to prey on the weaker peoples of the earth, on the false plea that they are spreading civilization, so long militarism is inexpugnable. If abolished to-day it will spring up anew to-morrow. If universal disarmament were decreed to-day, the aggressive West, bent on destroying the East, would to-morrow seize the first weapons at hand and apply its demoniac genius anew to inventing better ones. How symptomatic is the treatment of that issue in a huge flood that comes from the press! How little are we willing to acknowledge the source of the malady! We are not willing because we could not do so without confessing our

CIVILIZATION AND THE WAR

own sins.[1] When we consider the dealings of Europe with Asia and Africa, with the yellow man, the brown man and the black man, involuntarily there recurs to our mind the Biblical story of Ahab and of Naboth's vineyard. These weaker races are Naboth. Their lands and goods are Naboth's vineyard. Europe is Ahab, or perhaps we should say there are six Ahabs, half a dozen strong princes coveting Naboth's vineyard. And the claim of justice which they urge in the court of the world's opinion to-day is to a large extent the claim for an equal start in the race toward Naboth's vineyard, an equal chance to fall upon him and despoil him of his vineyard, an equal slice of his vineyard, or the right to the larger slice which one already has and the other covets. And there is no one who bethinks himself to ask the simple question, has then Naboth himself no rights against all these Ahabs? And is there any likelihood that they will ever learn to keep the peace among themselves until they cease the fight for that which legitimately belongs to none of them? Or is there, perhaps, to

[1] Germany may be the woman taken in adultery, but, taking into account only the history of the last ten years, who among the nations that point their finger at her is really warranted in casting the first stone?

be a tribunal at The Hague to pronounce upon the relative justice of claims each of which is tainted with an essential injustice? In one word, can there be international justice between the strong unless there be established international justice as between the strong and the weak? This is the question that keeps running in my head, and I am incessantly asking myself why it is that this point of view is slurred over.

There can be no change for the better in international relations until the poison is driven out of the system. The poison is the sinister spirit of aggression on the part of the strong races against the weak. Here there must be the change of policy, and an inner change of attitude to support the change in policy. The precious thing we call liberty, the right of self-direction, which is accorded to individuals, must be equally accorded to peoples. If they are too backward to use it, they must be trained to use it. If they are too weak to stand on their own feet, they must eventually be set on their own feet. *And the right intention here is everything.* Without self-government eventually for all there can be no true world civilization. The more advanced peoples in this

CIVILIZATION AND THE WAR

sense have an educational trust to fulfill toward the less advanced. They must be held to the fulfillment of it to the last letter. Order, security and justice between men and men in courts of law, are but initial gifts. These must not stand in the way of the exaction of the larger. Masters we are, and masters we intend to remain, is a formula to be rejected as little short of blasphemous in the light of the ultimate destiny of every member of the human race. Instead of excluding the possibility of ultimate withdrawal, the sole warrant for the exercise of power by a forward people over a backward people is the deliberate intent to extinguish that power at the earliest possible moment, to endow the subject race with freedom.

There is hope that the growth of democracy in England and elsewhere will exercise influence in this direction.[1] And the present policy of the United States in the Philippine Islands, if carried out as announced, will be the first example on a large scale of the successful ful-

[1] Though the hope is tempered with misgiving in view of the fact that the collective selfishness of democracies has shown itself to be as hard toward inferior races as that of kings and aristocrats. Consider the exploitation by France of the countries she had emancipated at the time of the Revolution, and the conduct of the American democracy toward the North American Indians and the negroes.

fillment on the part of a civilized people of the educative trust toward a less civilized people.

But the cup with which imperialism intoxicates the nations contains another ingredient not thus far mentioned, namely, the ferment that is active in pan-Germanism, pan-Slavism and in what is implied in the phrase, "The White Man's Burden," in all those movements in which the syllable "pan," meaning universal, is conjoined with some word like German, Slavic, etc., designating a limited circumscription. These hybrids, these universalized provincialisms, are a potent incentive in stimulating the aggression of the strong races upon the weak. And, as this aggression is the ultimate cause of the war, they must have a conspicuous place in explaining the war.

In every one of these instances racial conceit is at work, or an exaggerated predilection for the type of mentality characteristic of the people or group of peoples to which one belongs. Cramb says that the imprint of the English mind is to be stamped as widely as possible upon mankind. (Think of it, millions on millions of imitation Englishmen!) The Slavs hold a similar opinion with respect to their supposed mission, and the Germans express the idea with their usual intransigeant and laborious thoroughness. At a recent conference of German missionary societies, Professor Schröder quoted from Geibel the line

> Und nur am deutschen Wesen
> Soll einst die Welt genesen.

This may be freely rendered: "The German spirit is to be the world's salvation," or somewhat more literally, "By contact with the German nature the sick world shall regain its health." Professor Harnack, in a deeply serious address containing many notable thoughts, falls into the same vein when he represents the German people as a kind of modern Israel of culture, a Chosen People, and bases their title to consider themselves elect, oddly enough, on the very fact of their special gift for cosmopolitanism. It is the peculiar function of the Germans, he thinks, to absorb the best that is contained in the culture of other people, then to stamp it with their own mentality, and thus revalued to return it to its original sources. Here indeed we have the process of universalizing a provincialism carried to its extreme. Germany is the bee, distilling nectar from every flower, and turning it into honey for the world's consumption. He does not claim that culture is made in Germany. The gifts of culture are found among every people. But they need to be remade in Germany, reminted, standardized!

Now, it is of course true that the Germans are cosmopolitan as well as particularistic to an extraordinary degree. A kind of neo-Hellenism was at one time the rage in Germany, and still keeps its footing in the higher schools. They are eager and indefatigable translators, they have turned into their own tongue the best works of India and Persia. French literature has been profoundly studied by them. The merits of their Shakespearean scholarship cannot be denied. Yet it may very well be doubted whether this kind of cosmopolitanism, this sort of assimilation, is not itself a variety of imperialism in the realm of intellect—I mean the one-sided exploitation of Hellenism and the rest to enhance Germanism, the pressing of other minds into the German mold. And it is at least questionable whether the Greeks of the Periclean age would altogether recognize their image as reflected in German neo-Hellenism, and whether Shakespeare would feel quite at home if he were to wander through some of the

CIVILIZATION AND THE WAR

German commentaries on his plays. The right of reinterpretation after one's own fashion is not disputed. Such reinterpretation is inevitable. What must be rejected is the pretension that the Teutonic interpretation shall set the fashion for all mankind.

⌈The spurious universalism with which we are dealing, indicated by the prefix "pan," is a most insidious sort of imperialism, imperialism in the inner field, the field of mind. It is an infringement of the right to a distinctive mental complexion which belongs to every people and every group of peoples. The psychic type, the mental pattern, of the Chinese differs from that of the Hindoos; that of the Hindoos is unlike that of the Persians; that of the French unlike that of the Italians, etc. Every nation has not only the right but the duty of developing into utmost explicitness its native gifts in the interest of the diversity of the human species, and of the ultimate harmonization of the complex differences. And where, as among the backward races, the psychic type is still latent, it is the duty of the forward races to assist in maturing it. They may not crush it by superimposing their own.⌋

And there is one further capital consideration which must be brought forward if I am to make my thought in this matter entirely clear. Every one of the psychic types has its grave defects as well as its excellences. There is not one that can set up as a model for all the rest, because there is not one that is free from serious flaws, not one that does not stand in need of thoroughgoing correction and modification. If I have pleaded for the mental independence of the different peoples, I can express my entire thought only by emphasizing as a necessary supplement the indispensable mental interdependence of these peoples. Now the faults of each are most mercilessly revealed by observing the effect produced by a people who stand for a certain psychic type, or type of civilization, on other peoples. If you would discover, for instance, the defects of the English type, study the effect the Englishman produces on the people of India. If you would discover the defects of the German type, study the revolt which Teutonism is conjuring up against itself amongst the nations at the present moment. If you would discover the defects of American democracy, note the relative discredit into which democracy has fallen among many of the advanced thinkers abroad in consequence of the weaknesses of democracy as illustrated in the United States. If you would obtain a realizing impression of the defects of our Western civilization as a whole, consider the devastating effect it is producing upon the life of the East: the undermining of Oriental religious ideals without any adequate substitute offered; the harm done to the family ideals and social ideals of Eastern peoples by the abrupt intrusion of our individualism; the sudden forcing upon them of our mechanical science and mechanical inventions, of our whole mechanical conception of life, without relation to their ancient mental habits and traditions.

In the moral development of individuals, independence and interdependence are correlative terms. It is the same in the moral development of nations. To the individual we say: If you would be a full-grown personality, work out the distinctive best that is in you. But, in order so to do, look to your radiations. Observe the effect you produce upon others. Keep in view as your steadfast aim to bring out the best that is in them, and in attempting to do this you will inevitably find out where you are weak and why you are weak, where you fail and why you fail; you will be challenged to correct your defects, and thus attain to self-development.

It is the same with peoples. Let the peoples remember that they as nations are members of one another, and that not merely individual men as individual men are members of one another. Let each people endeavor to assist in bringing out the psychic possibilities of its fellow-members in the universal bond. By so doing it will most certainly discover its own faults and be incited to correct them.

Thus *national humility,* compatible with proper confidence in a national destiny, is the keynote of international ethics. And international ethics is the foundation of international law. And international law is the only sure basis for international justice and peace. Not the pride of any people, in its poor conceit esteeming itself the torch-bearer for all the rest, or the model; but the humility of each people, the consciousness of defect, is the fundamental condition of human peace and progress. In the last analysis there must be a bond of high and pure self-interest to tie the nations together. That highest and purest self-interest is interest in the development of each nation's own national personality, as conditioned by and accomplished through its beneficent influence in multiplying the variety and beauty of the psychic types among mankind.[1]

But if such be the goal and the way of progress, how distant seems the goal, how long the way! The profound depression, the melancholy, the pessimism, produced by the war in many quarters has been due to an egregious self-deception. It had been believed that we were very much further along the road than we actually are. Then suddenly there came this rude shock, and we recognized to our mortification that we are still in the early stages of spiritual development, "at the cock-crowing," as Emerson puts it. But if this be so, what ground is

---

[1] The difference between English and American liberalism and the view indicated above depends on the negative conception of freedom in the one case and the positive conception of freedom in the other. The ideal of even the most radical liberals stresses independence without due weight on interdependence. The ideal condition of nations is conceived of as one in which they dwell in juxtaposition, each without interference from its neighbors, realizing its own ends. This is the same idea of liberty for peoples as Mill described and desired for individuals. The mutual assimilation of the products of culture, the enjoyment by all of what is produced by each, is quite possible under such a scheme. But the idea of positive freedom or of interdependence goes far beyond these limits. It puts the chief stress on the self-development of nations, as of individuals, through the effort to assist in the distinctive development of others.

there for believing that progress is attainable at all? This is a topic on which it remains to say a word in closing.

The evidence of history is inconclusive in respect to progress. There never has been an advance but it was attended by serious loss. The facts of evolution likewise fall far short of establishing a proof, or even a balance of probabilities in favor of future progress. The story of evolution as we have it in our hands consists of the middle pages torn out of a book, and of this book we cannot possibly reconstruct the beginning nor forecast the end. The belief in progress, like the Kingdom of Heaven, cometh not by observation, no, nor by the method of observation. The faith in progress is not a scientific generalization at all but a moral postulate. It is a morally indispensable hypothesis if there is to be progress. It is a faith not to be inferred from facts, but one that creates the facts which are to justify it; or rather, to speak carefully, for the facts never justify the faith, it is the act itself of creation; it is the kind of sublime satisfaction experienced in the effort that justifies the effort.

If anyone taking the attitude of the scientific discoverer were to ask at any given moment in regard to himself: Is it likely that I shall be a better man ten years hence than I am now? he would presumably realize that it is impossible for him to make a prediction one way or the other; and if he were to venture to do so at all, he would probably be compelled to take an unfavorable view of his future. He would have to take into consideration his frequent lapses and indefensible shortcomings, the evil strains, perhaps, in his heredity, his unpropitious environment, the lack of that coöperation on the part of others which is so helpful toward the attainment of moral improvement. Yet if he be a person of sound moral sense, he will also realize that the right attitude to take is not that of the scientific discoverer, but of a man endowed with will. He will realize that what is wanted of him is not prediction but resolution. He will resolve then to be a better person than he has been, using the opportunities that favor him, mastering the untoward circumstances as best he may.

It is the same with mankind. For each generation the question of progress is not one of fact or of inference, but of resolution. Will mankind after us achieve progress? We cannot tell. Shall we of the present generation advance morally? We cannot predict. We do not know. Ought we to progress? Assuredly, yes. Can we? Yes, indeed, because we ought. Then let us use our best endeavor that we actually may. Progress signifies the gradual approximation of civilization to the moral ideal. Progress is ever a present purpose. Progress is not summarized in external conditions, save instrumentally. Progress consists in a certain attitude of mind existing among the rational beings who occupy this earth, and in the expression of this attitude in their wills. Progress of this kind is possible at every moment in the private and public history of men. The faith in it is founded in the experience of it.

VI

THE MORAL AWAKENING OF THE WEALTHY

THE Emperor Augustus, according to the story in Suetonius, was displeased with one of his generals who had jeopardized the safety of the army to gain only an insignificant advantage. He compared this general to a man who uses a golden hook to catch fish, risking the loss of what all the fish he could catch would not replace. Such is he who risks the loss of self-respect in the pursuit of wealth.

It is certain that in the commercial world a change is taking place suggestive of a moral awakening, or at least half-awakening. Nothing nowadays is more common than to hear men of affairs admit, and even proclaim with some emphasis, that they have seen "a new light." What they evidently mean is that the methods of doing business which they practiced a little while ago without scruple now seem to them wrong. The Sinaitic Commandments are receiving additions. Thou shalt not contribute to the campaign expenses of political parties from the money of policyholders whose wishes in the matter have not been consulted; thou shalt not play the rôle of a "dummy" director. At a meeting recently held where large financial interests were represented, one of the leading men present declared that hereafter a more conscientious respect must be shown for the interests of stockholders, and that corporations must meet the just demands of the public by rendering more adequate service in return for their franchises.

The mere onlooker, the literary man, or the student of manners, who has not been subjected himself to the temptations which the engrossing pursuit of wealth brings with it, may perhaps exclaim in some amazement that the "new light" that men engaged in "big business" profess to have seen is not new light at all, and that the supposed additions to the Decalogue are in effect comprised in the plain old commandment, "Thou shalt not steal." Nevertheless, a new sensitiveness to elementary notions of right and wrong, under conditions which tend to obscure them, does constitute a distinct social advance. There has been a moral awakening, though it is far from complete, and by no means general. Some of the worst practices continue in full force. In a recent report issued by the Federal Government it is stated that a labor day of twelve hours still prevails in some of the principal industries of the United States. Despite the fact that forty states have passed child-labor laws, these excellent laws are in many cases quite imperfectly enforced, and in the backward states the remorseless exploitation of an army of child-workers, numbering many thousands, goes on unchecked. It needs no lengthy argument nor multiplicity of instances to prove that the millennium is not yet in sight, or to demonstrate that the spirit of greed, when dislodged from one of its strongholds, is quick to entrench itself at other vantage points, often less exposed to attack. And yet, can we be mistaken in the feeling that the "breath of God" is moving over the waters? Is there not a moral freshness in the air; a change, or the premonition of a change? At any rate, we are justified in assuming that there is, and doing what we can to promote it by testing the moral standards themselves by a frank, though we hope not censorious or pretentious, discussion of the grounds which men of large fortune sometimes advance to justify the prodigious inequalities of possession that characterize and disturb modern society.

The outstanding fact that must strike everyone who stops to think is the broken self-consciousness of the thoughtful rich. The social atmosphere around us is charged with the idea of the fundamental equality of all human beings. The wealthy, as citizens of a democracy, have themselves imbibed this idea, and are subject to its influence. On the other hand, as the owners of excessive wealth they are examples of the greatest inequalities of fortune that have ever existed on earth. The position is anomalous beyond description. There is democracy on the one hand, with its belief in equality, and the actual industrial situation, with its outcome of enormous inequality, on the other. The man of wealth consequently tends to be divided into two inharmonious selves: one a democratic self, sympathizing with general equality; the other the more egotistical self, clinging to privileges all the more tightly because they are being challenged. And the result is this broken self-consciousness, the loss of that inward whole-

MORAL AWAKENING OF THE WEALTHY

ness which is so indispensable to self-respect and contentment. A man who absolutely knows his own mind, who stands firmly on his feet, who never questions, and will not allow others to question his privileges, who believes himself entitled to the best there is, regardless of others, be he king or nobleman, may not be a personality to our liking, but we can hardly refuse him the tribute of a certain respect. Whatever else he may or may not be, such a person is at any rate all-of-a-piece. And the best members of the privileged orders of the past were of this description. They held with Plato that some men are endowed at birth with a golden nature, others with a silver nature, and others with a copper nature; and they believed very stoutly that those who possessed the golden nature should sit on the golden thrones and should have opened to them the golden gates of opportunity. Some of the faces that look out upon us from the portraits of Venetian or English aristocracy are of this type. "Now a house divided against itself cannot stand," neither can a self that is divided against itself persist in this condition. Attempts will be made in any case to get relief from the strain of being drawn in two directions, and com-

THE WORLD CRISIS AND ITS MEANING

promises of one kind or another will be the result.

One of these compromises is the so-called "square deal." As a popular cry, and as a protest against some of the more extreme commercial iniquities, the motto of the "square deal" is serving a useful purpose. But still it is a doctrine which does not go to the heart of the matter. It does not at all criticize nor correct the desire for inordinate accumulation; it rather gives it its blessing, insisting merely that the game be played decently, according to the rules. The standard of commercial ethics, therefore, that is put into the phrase the "square deal" will never suffice to curb the fierce, passionate impulse of greed, for it allows and encourages those very impulses, only bidding them keep within the rules of the game. It says in effect: Get rich, as rich as possible, but be exceedingly scrupulous in the methods of which you avail yourself; seek to achieve an inequality of possessions which will raise you high above your fellows, but at the same time observe the laws that have their sole foundation in the idea of human equality. Is not this giving with one hand and withdrawing with the other? Enkindling in men a fierce thirst and

MORAL AWAKENING OF THE WEALTHY

at the same time forbidding them to quench it?

Another compromise between plutocracy and democracy is profit-sharing, and of this we have an extraordinary example in the plan recently adopted by Mr. Henry Ford. It appears that some twenty-six thousand wage-earners are to share in the advantages of the scheme, that five dollars a day is to be the minimum wage, and that an expected income of perhaps ten million dollars is to be divided equally between the employing company and its employees. The generous motive that inspired this act has everywhere received proper recognition. Indeed, it is hard to see how anyone can help rejoicing in a project which promises immediate benefit to so large a number of persons, and which seems to be dictated by humanitarian motives. Now this profit-sharing plan as outlined is, I take it, the product of three factors: (1) The democratic atmosphere, and its pressure on the individual. (2) The plutocratic fact, inconsistent with democracy, of millions of dollars of annual income. (3) The personal benevolence of the man. For this last, and for the extent to which he has yielded to the democratic pressure enveloping him, he certainly deserves unstinted credit. Of ten millions he proposes to relinquish five to the wage-earners, though he might have retained them for himself, without the condemnation of the law or the censure of public opinion. He seems to be influenced by the consideration that the quota of the profits coming to himself was too large, that he ought to share it with those who coöperate with him in creating the product. He has certainly outstripped average public opinion. He has set the pace for a more advanced public opinion; and already others are beginning to follow in his footsteps.

But by this action of his he has raised a tremendous question which has nothing to do with his individual merit, but with the system of ideas from which his action springs. It seems that he wishes to do the right thing by his employees, that he is setting out to apply the notion of "rightness" to the share which the employer should abandon to his employees and to that which he may keep himself. The searching question forced upon us is, granted that he is generous in giving up five million dollars to his people, would he be just in keeping five million for himself? Or, to relieve the discussion of the unpleasant personal note, is

MORAL AWAKENING OF THE WEALTHY

an employer who is generous therefore just? It used to be held that to be generous is to be more than just, but it seems possible to be generous and less than just—that is, generous so far as one's impulses are concerned, and yet lacking in justice in the broader sense of the term. Is the successful kind of big business man entitled to the large income which under present conditions keeps flooding in upon him? If he is entitled to it, then we ask on what grounds? We want to know what these grounds are and examine them. It is of deep interest to all of us to find out what is right in this matter. And it must assuredly be of supreme interest to the wealthy themselves to find out what is right in this matter if, indeed, they wish to be entirely awake, morally speaking, and not to remain in a state of semi-drowsiness.

A man of large means and influential position as an employer said to me not long ago: "I do not care to make more money. I have all the money I want. I am interested in discovering what is right in industrial relations." That is the finest and most thrilling word I have heard in many a day. If such should prove to be the temper of the employers of labor in

THE WORLD CRISIS AND ITS MEANING

America, there is hope of effectual progress in the world of capital and labor.

But in such inquiries as this there is a certain fallacy against which we ought to be well on our guard. It is that of confusing what is right with what is immediately feasible. It is often laid down that the present mixed system of industrial plutocracy in a political democracy is the only feasible plan. We need, it is said, the men of exceptional energy and daring initiative to build our railroads, to carry out schemes of commercial expansion, to make new inventions workable; and the dazzling prospect of huge profits is the only motive sufficiently powerful to call out the exercise of their abilities. This argument in defense of things as they are may be true or not. There certainly is another side to the story; but whether true or false it is irrelevant. The argument concerns what is actually or supposedly practicable at the present moment. We are concerned to know what is right. To measure the right by what is immediately feasible is to be afflicted with moral strabismus, or, in plain English, moral squinting. To squint is to have the eye directed to two different objects at the same moment. To see straight is to look first at the

MORAL AWAKENING OF THE WEALTHY

one and then at the other. To see straight in moral issues is to look first at the right in its pure, clear outlines, and then to consider in how far the present state of things may gradually be approximated to the right. We ask, then, are the great rewards of wealth that come to the organizers of industrial victory justified? And, if so, on what grounds?

Of the reasons commonly alleged, some may be dismissed in short order. Thus, if it is said that large fortunes are needed as reservoirs from which investment-capital may be recruited, the answer to this is that the process of accumulation would yield still better results if there were fewer large and a greater number of moderate fortunes, the deposits in the savings banks being evidence in point.

For the possession of wealth far in excess of possible legitimate need is a constant temptation to unprofitable expenditure and hence to waste of capital. Reports from England recently described a kind of fairy fête held in the underground picture gallery of a castle owned by the Duke of Portland. This gallery, it was said, had been constructed at an expense of thirty-five million dollars. The accuracy of the figures may be disputed, as sensational news. But the story has symbolic, if not literal, veracity, as calling attention to the needless and harmful diminution of capital which under the present system is constantly going on.

A second argument is equally flimsy, namely, that there must be concentration of wealth in order that there may be philanthropy. The answer to this is that if wealth were less concentrated there would be less need of philanthropy, and also that in so far as charitable giving would still be needed, the total sum of small gifts would produce adequate amounts, and, moreover, would mean far more in terms of the self-sacrifice of the many givers.

A third argument which sticks obstinately in the mind of many intelligent people is that "the laborer is worthy of his hire," the laborer in this case being the successful merchant or manufacturer. The prosperity of the business, it is said, is due to his sagacity, his mental grasp, his strenuous application. He works hard and often longer hours than the wage-earners whom he employs. It is true that the operatives in the mills and the mines likewise toil day by day, and that their work is less agreeable, but what would all their toil be worth were it not for the directing mind that

MORAL AWAKENING OF THE WEALTHY

guides the processes of production and profitably places the finished product? When labor organizations in their manifestoes speak of themselves as if they were the sole producers of wealth, are they not ignoring the part played by the directing minds, is it not as if the private soldiers should arrogate to themselves the credit of a successful campaign, setting aside the claims of those who planned and conducted it? In short, is it not fair that the men of superior ability should reap a reward proportionate to their greater ability?

The decisive answer to this is that the men of superior ability are asking to be paid twice over, and it is not fair for anyone to be paid twice over.[1]

For they are paid already, and more than paid, in the mere possession of their superior abilities. What, is it not then an enormous gift and privilege to possess exceptional brain power? Carlyle had his fling at the multitude in speaking of the millions of the people of

[1] The question here is what is *right*, not what, under economic laws of demand and supply, men of superior gifts are able to exact. I waive two other points of extreme importance, such as the part played by mere shrewdness, or even base unscrupulousness in the accumulation of fortunes, and the glaring injustice of the inheritance of excessive wealth by those who have done nothing to produce it.

England as for the most part fools. We need not take his exaggerated, pessimistic view; but certainly it is true that while the average of intelligence among civilized peoples may be rising, men of exceptional intelligence, of superior brain power, are few and far between. It should be remembered that this brain power which they possess has come to them at birth as a gift. They may develop it by industry and application, but the power itself is a free gift. All the industry in the world would not help them if there were not the endowment at the start. Again, this gift, this endowment, is a social product. For ages on ages generations of men have been building it up. Like the coral reef, according to the familiar comparison, the mentality of the present day is the topmost layer reposing on myriads of mental acquisitions beneath. But only the elect few rise above the level; only the few inherit, in a conspicuous degree, the power produced by humanity during all the preceding ages. They are paid, I would repeat, and more than paid, by their exceeding share of the mental capital. Can they stand up in the court of reason and demand, on this very account also, an excessive share of the money capital? This indeed would be with

MORAL AWAKENING OF THE WEALTHY

a vengeance "unto him that hath shall be given."

For my part, I confess that I have long since given up the attempt to establish an equation between the just deserts of the worker, the head-worker or the hand-worker, on the one hand, and wages, salary or income on the other. No such equation is possible. Every endeavor to construct one is unsound. The proportion between work done and income received will have to be based on a totally different principle, and the word "reward" must be entirely expunged from the vocabulary of economic justice. The principle I mean is sustentation and not remuneration. The just principle is that which sustains the worker at the highest possible pitch of efficiency in doing his work, not that which rewards or remunerates him for doing it. The reward of the work, so far as there is any, is or must be in the work itself.[1]

---

[1] In popular discussion, and even in more scholarly treatises, the ideas of merit and origination are often confused. The originator, or producer, of a thing is supposed to be the rightful owner. It is his own work, in the sense that he made it, therefore his own in the sense of proprietorship. This argument is used on both sides, by laborers, as well as by employers. The laborers insist on the quantity of their work; the employers, on the increment of quality which they add

THE WORLD CRISIS AND ITS MEANING

But if this be so, how strikingly in excess of right and justice are the multiplying incomes of the wealthy at the present time. How far beyond what they can possibly require to sustain them at the highest mark of efficiency! And how gross is the discrepancy between the haphazard distribution of riches under the operation of the law of demand and supply and the kind of allotment which would satisfy the genuine demands of fairness and due proportion! So that we are bound to say that the claim still often put forth on behalf of the present assignment of material goods that it somehow is, or somehow can be made out to be, right

to the product, and on which its economic value depends. But "own" in the one sense does not justify "own" in the other. Origination does not of itself confer proprietorship, else the inventor of a new machine would be entitled to the total increase of wealth produced by means of it, and the discoverer of a new remedy for disease would be entitled to a commission from all the fees of the physicians who utilize it. Besides, there are two other objections. The product brought forth by the joint effort of laborer and employer is one in which the increments of value added by each are indistinguishably blended; and, as has just been shown, the higher mental ability itself is a social product, the net residuum of the efforts of past generations. So that even if origination were a title to proprietorship, as it is not, if "own" in the one sense justified "own" in the other, the origin would have to be traced back to mankind at large, mankind would have to be recognized as the owner, not the individual *able man of to-day.*

has really not a leg to stand on. Every ground on which it has been rested, when scrutinized, turns out to be untenable and delusive, and in the forum of reason must be rejected. If, indeed, we take our stand on brute force, if we assert that might makes right, and that in the struggle for existence the weaker must go to the wall, that is another matter. But then we divest ourselves of our higher humanity and step down to lower levels.

Even the contention that, aside from the question of merit, the magnitude of the social services rendered by men in big business should be reflected, if not rewarded, in the magnitude of their fortunes, cannot be sustained. Comparisons are challenged which at once invalidate it. Certainly Pasteur, in respect to the magnitude of his services, outshines all the clever financiers, the heads of corporations and the rest, even in the value in dollars and cents of the social service he performed. Huxley estimated that Pasteur saved France a sum probably equal to the entire war indemnity paid by that country after the war with Germany, by the series of discoveries which saved the silk industry, improved the wine-making industry, expelled the cattle scourge, and made possible the rescue of countless human lives from the ravages of infectious diseases. We should also think of the great physicists who by their researches have paved the way for the use of electricity in industry, the great chemists who have transformed certain large branches of modern industry, the inventors who never reaped the material fruit of their inventions, and it may be permissible to add, the scholars, the artists, the teachers, who have enriched human life by ennobling it.

Indeed, the moment the argument of social service is pressed, that moment the demand for large money compensation is condemned. Between the magnitude of a real social service, and the magnitude of a pile of bank notes, there is no relation. The two are incommensurable. And if finally it be said that, right or wrong, we must have industrial progress, and that the hope of immense riches is the only "bait at which our men of enterprise will bite," that it pays society to overpay them, I believe this, too, to be an error. We are not to think as meanly of our industrial captains as those who undertake to speak for them seem to think of them. Closer acquaintance with some of them, at all events, reveals fine grain underneath a

MORAL AWAKENING OF THE WEALTHY

sometimes hard exterior, and generosities and public spirit dormant because they have never been called out. A talent or gift of any kind is a fire in a man's bones, a pressure from within seeking a vent. Give it a chance to effectuate itself, and the man is content. Give to the man of teeming brain, untiring will and planful imagination a field within which to display his power, and he will, in the end, ask no greater boon. A salary such as is paid to a competent railroad president, or less, will suffice him.

So much for the right as I view it. Let us now turn to the feasible. We have seen reason to conclude that the present state of things is not right, but wrong. The man having a superfluous income, even if he conforms to the stricter standard of business ethics, is in a false position. How shall he square himself? He is a plutocrat in the midst of a democracy. If he is morally sensitive he will suffer under the strain of a broken self-consciousness. How can he regain inward wholeness, how maintain his self-respect? There are two ways open. The one touches his personal habits, the other the line he may follow in helping to alter present economic conditions in conformity with a better social ideal. Let me speak of the former way because of its immediate practical bearings.

There is one thing obviously that a man can do if he is over-rich. He can live as if he were not so. Marcus Aurelius said that a man can be a man even in a palace. He meant, of course, that though as emperor he could not avoid living in a palace, he might still live simply in such surroundings. A private citizen does not need to live in anything like a palace. Even if financially he can afford to do so, he cannot morally afford to do so. He can live instead in a modest house on a modest scale.

Granted that it is not possible, by act of legislature, to set effectual limits to the amount of wealth a man may acquire, why should a high-minded person wait for the law to compel what he can freely do of his own accord? If the pursuit of unlimited wealth, and also the enjoyment of it, are injurious, why should he not set his own limit, and decide when he has enough?

Into the social reform literature of the day there has crept a tone of bitterness against the rich, which is due in part to deep moral resentments, but also to a false estimate of the happi-

MORAL AWAKENING OF THE WEALTHY

ness enjoyed by the rich. It is naïvely imagined that they are supremely enviable; that they have obtained the best things, and that, except for the selfishness which prevents them from sharing with others, nothing much better could be desired than the life they are living. But the business of wealth-getting, and of wealth-enjoyment, when viewed at close range, turns out to be a very different matter. Its effect is almost inevitably unfortunate, not only on society at large, but on the mind and character of the wealthy themselves. There is the grimness of the struggle, the sinister methods often stooped to, and there is besides another retroactive effect not so commonly remarked, but quite as important, namely, the gradual enfeeblement of the capacity for the disinterested appraisement of values which is due to the persistent habit of self-interested calculation. It is as certain as anything can be that the appreciation and enjoyment of all that is really best in human existence—knowledge, beauty, virtue —depends upon a disinterested attitude of mind. But to this the pursuit of wealth is distinctly unfavorable. The man of large wealth can, indeed, promote the progress of science, but he can hardly enter into the scientist's enthusiasms. He may be a collector of fine pictures, and hang them up in his gallery, but he can hardly, except under favor of exceptional endowment, compete with the artist in the understanding of them, or the delight in them. If he is the typical wealth-getter, of the kind we find in America, his mind will be too restless, too preoccupied, to dwell with sincere absorption on these fine creations. A disinterested spirit is almost as necessary to the appreciation as it is to the production of the masterpieces. And if this holds of wealth-getting, there are other obstacles to the more desirable life connected with wealth possession. Too much time and attention must be given to the blind pomps, the heavy ritual, with which wealth celebrates its continuous festivals. The temptation is too great, especially for the young, to whom inherited wealth is frequently a veritable curse, to indulge in unwholesome pleasures, or to allow the mind to decline upon the minor and softer enjoyments at the expense of the higher, the more virile and lasting. Instead of envying the possessors of great wealth as if the best life were at their command, it were better, on the contrary, to combat this strange delusion, not only for the sake of the wealthy minority, but

MORAL AWAKENING OF THE WEALTHY

also for the sake of American society as a whole.[1]

I would urge the principle of *self-limitation in regard to wealth.* This is not a solution of the social problem—I am not now discussing this; I am discussing the problem of the broken self-consciousness of the plutocrat in a democracy, and asking how this person can save his soul alive; how he can do so now, in advance of the coming of the social reconstruction on which we may have set our hearts. And I would insist that he can at all events lead, not the simple life, but what I should prefer to call the essential life; that he can take out of the share of wealth that comes to him only so much as he needs to realize the essentials of a truly human existence, to maintain himself at the highest standard of efficiency in doing his work. This is not to say that he should assimilate his condition to that of the poor. For, if we say

[1] Attention has been concentrated upon the very wealthy for the sake of distinctness. But persons of moderate fortune, and even the multitude of the more or less indigent, are to a large extent in this country victims of the same false appraisement. The desire for unbounded wealth exists even where there is no hope for gratification, and the venom of unsatisfied desire infects the mind. My argument is directed, not against a few, but against a mistaken ideal which to a great extent permeates throughout American society.

167

THE WORLD CRISIS AND ITS MEANING

that, where shall we draw the line? There are gradations and degradations among those whom in a general way we call the poor. There are depths below depths. Shall he descend to the very lowest level of want and nakedness, so as to be superior to none? But there are also gradations above gradations, and the precise level at which he must halt his own conscience can alone determine. Certain things he will need and use without scruple, in order to represent and maintain the standard of civilization in his own person. But hard and fast rules in a matter of this sort, in default of scientific investigations, which have hardly been begun, cannot be given. The right spirit will lead to right decisions. We have thus considered what is feasible under present circumstances in one aspect, so far as personal expenditure is concerned. We have proposed as a general truth that a man should spend only up to the limit of his proper human needs, devoting the surplus to the promotion of progressive social movements in the right direction. Such movements are always languishing for support. There is never sufficient financial support to carry them on with the best possible results. There is no occasion for embarrassment as to excel-

MORAL AWAKENING OF THE WEALTHY

lent objects that cry for adequate assistance.[1]

But there is one more question which should be mentioned here. A man, let us say, of exceptionally fine temper has seen the vision of the right, in contrast with the economic system under which we are actually working. He is an employer of labor, and the head of a large industrial plant. His conscience smites him. He says to himself: The position I occupy is wrong; the privileges I enjoy I am not in real justice entitled to. Suppose that he asks our advice. Shall we advise him to abdicate his position, to wash his hands of the whole bad business, making way for others, perhaps less scrupulous than himself? Surely we shall not let him off so easily. We have been speaking of the privileged class, and have perhaps conveyed the impression that only the rich are the privileged. The privileged class, however, includes many who are not at all wealthy. There is hardly one of us who does not in some way enjoy privileges to which he has no absolute claim. A teacher in a university, for instance, subsisting on a small salary, has an inestimable

[1] Everyone should set aside a surplus for such purposes. It is better to curtail even one's legitimate needs rather than forego the moral uplift, or neglect the moral duty of contributing to the general good.

privilege, the privilege of leisure, of undisturbed communion with the best thinking of past and present, the privilege of implanting in the minds of the young seeds that may sprout later on into still more valid knowledge. I am a teacher in a university and I recognize my privileges. But I know very well that among the uneducated whom on my way to the university I pass in the streets, there are doubtless not a few who, if they had had the opportunities that fortune threw in my way, would be as well fitted, and better fitted, to hold the place which I occupy. Am I therefore to cede my place to them, seeing that as a matter of fact they are uneducated, and have not had the opportunities, because if they had had them they would make the better teachers? On the contrary, I am to stay at my post, I am to do the best I can with my opportunities, regarding them in the light of responsibilities, but also helping as far as in my power lies to promote an order of society in which there shall be a less inadequate selection of the talented. It is the same with the artist. Possibly there are hundreds of persons who could paint even better pictures than he if they had had the training. But none the less he is to keep his place and continue seeking to

MORAL AWAKENING OF THE WEALTHY

produce the vital art that gives ease to the human spirit and vigor to the imagination. The same finally is true of the head of an industrial plant. Among the workmen whom he passes as he goes through his factories there are probably some, and in the city around there are certainly not a few, who have the same or better ability than he, and who would perform his function in industry as well or better than he if the circumstances of their early life had not closed the door of opportunity in their faces. But that is no reason for installing the untrained, who have not had the opportunities, in his place, in the name of a specious democracy. That is no reason for him to step down and invite the mass of untrained workmen to run his works. It is a reason for him to stay where he is, to fulfill his office to the utmost of his ability, and in the social spirit; that is to say, to use his opportunities in order to prepare the way for a social order better and more just than that which now is.

VII

AN ETHICAL PROGRAM OF SOCIAL REFORM

IN addressing this plea to the wealthy we have in mind only persons of sufficient moral sensitiveness and reflectiveness to realize the anomaly of their situation, and to suffer distress in consequence. The first step to take, if they would set themselves right, is to live in the midst of superfluous wealth as if they were not the possessors of it; that is, to take for their own use only what they require for the essentials of a civilized life, and to regard the rest as a deposit for the general good of which they themselves are not to be the beneficiaries.

But self-restriction in spending is only the initial, indispensable condition. A more serious step remains to be taken; a far mightier problem rises into view. "The world is out of joint." It always has been, and it always will be more or less, though the "more or less"

AN ETHICAL PROGRAM OF SOCIAL REFORM

makes a difference. Nor is it a "cursed spite" that we should be born to set it right, as young *Hamlet* opines. The business of setting things right is a malignant curse only to megalomaniacs who believe that the whole burden rests on them, or to fanatics who expect that by some specific remedy of which they believe themselves to possess the secret the long working day of mankind can be shortened to a single hour. The task of setting things right, never achieved, yet never therefore to be remitted, is itself that which makes living worth while. Could we ever arrive we should desist from further effort. But to live is to put forth effort. It is effort that counts, not result, except in so far as result inspires and instigates to further effort. The dying words of Buddha are forever memorable: "Strive without ceasing."

But in what direction shall we strive? Or what scheme of social reconstruction shall we adopt, if any, from among the many that clamor for acceptance? There must evidently be some plan, or else our efforts are foredoomed to be feeble and confused. Some distinct end must be set up toward which to direct effort. Our definition of it may be never so imperfect

THE WORLD CRISIS AND ITS MEANING

and provisional; still, such as it is, it must serve as a guide and goal.[1]

I think our main concern should be adequately to define the word "human." Everyone will probably agree that the immediate task of social reform is to bring forward the "human factor" in industry, to secure due respect and consideration for human beings in their *human quality*. But what is the human quality? For that purpose we may use the rough classification: things, animals, human beings. First, then, a man should not be treated like a thing. Labor is not a mere commodity to be bought and sold like cloth. "A man's a man for a' that." The circumstance that he is a factory operative should not obscure the more pertinent fact that he is a man.[2]

It is true a man is also a thing. The law of gravitation acts on him as it does on any mere stone. But the thing nature which he shares with inanimate objects is not the characteristically human nature in him. If we propose to

[1] The test of the right end is that it shall be of such a nature as to sting us to new effort, being itself the womb of new conceptions of itself, as of an end without end.

[2] Political economy has had some difficulty in extricating itself from the notion that labor is just a commodity like any other, and, indeed, it has not yet entirely freed itself from this pernicious fallacy.

174

AN ETHICAL PROGRAM OF SOCIAL REFORM

bring the human factor forward, we must beware how we look upon a man as a thing. If you look upon people in a certain way, you will be sure to treat them accordingly! *The keynote of social reform is to bring about the right way of looking upon fellowmen.*

In the next place, every man has an animal nature. He has a bodily organism like animals. He is sensitive to pain and pleasure; he hungers and thirsts. But again his animal nature is not the characteristically human quality in him. We should therefore beware how we express our respect for men in terms of the satisfaction of their merely animal wants. This is in no slight degree the error of the social betterment movements of our time. The leaders of these movements undoubtedly recognize that there is something higher in man than the animal side of him, but they seem to have no distinct or clarified conception of what that higher something is. And hence their plea for the uplift of the disadvantaged is overweighted on the side of securing conditions that shall provide completer contentment for men's animal wants. The laborer, it is said, should not be underfed. The wages he receives, being insufficient to furnish him with adequate nourishment, should be increased. But, neither should an ox or a horse be underfed! The laborer should not be overtaxed. The hours of labor, therefore, should be shortened. But neither should a horse or ox be overworked! The laborer should be properly housed; so should domestic animals! Indeed, the stables on some model farms compare favorably, in point of cleanliness and hygienic conditions, with even the improved tenements in our larger cities.

This argument is that which *Shylock* uses for equal treatment by his Christian fellow-townsmen. "If you prick me, do I not bleed?"—so does any animal. "If you poison me, do I not die?"—so does any animal. And it is a slippery argument, leading, in his case, to a heinous conclusion: "If you wrong me, shall I not revenge?"

In escaping from the thing view of human beings we are in real danger of falling into the animal view of them. The idea of justice will have no place in our treatment of them. Compassion may enter in, or self-interest, but not justice. Animals are not our moral equals, and justice is founded on moral equality. I do not insinuate that the idea of justice is absent from the minds of social reformers of the class I

AN ETHICAL PROGRAM OF SOCIAL REFORM

have described. It is the driving motive that impels their exertions. But they have no definite notion of the human quality on which the claim for equal treatment depends. And therefore the idea of justice tends to play over into the material satisfactions in which it is expressed, to be merged in them, to be smothered by them. The light that shines on the path of reform in the beginning grows faint, and the bitter struggle of class against class ensues. The voluminous selfishness of the mass is arrayed against the selfishness of strong individuals.[1] The question, What is the distinctively human nature in any human being? is exigent of an explicit answer.

A number of answers have been tried in the past. That of Christian theology was one. According to this the human entity in human nature is that something which Christ came to save. It is called Soul. The soul, however, is irretrievably lost through sin. All men are indeed equal in the sense that each, like his neigh-

[1] In intention these movements are hedonistic rather than materialistic. Education, recreation, esthetic pleasure, figure as desiderata in the social betterment programs. Opportunity is demanded for the exercise of the so-called higher faculties. We shall presently consider whether "the higher faculties" without the conception of the highest can serve our purpose.

bor, possesses a soul. But the soul is destined to perdition unless it becomes the subject of redemption. Yet redemption is impossible except through faith in Christ, and faith, alas! is imparted only by supernatural grace. Supernatural grace plays like a searchlight across the world, touching here and there a human being, and illumining him, but leaving the vast majority in darkness.

Another less controversial and more obvious answer is that which identifies the distinctively human attribute with the so-called higher faculties—the faculty for language, the ability to form abstract ideas: in brief, reason. Of this view Aristotle was the chief exponent in ancient times. To determine the essential nature of any species, his method was to ascertain the singular attribute in respect to which that species stands out and excels all others. Thus the specific excellence of the lion is strength, of the eagle flight, of the antelope speed, while the specific excellence of man, that which reveals his essential human nature, according to the great thinker Aristotle, is thinking. And, of course, when he says this, he means thinking to good purpose, thinking correctly, thinking in such a way as to achieve the high-

AN ETHICAL PROGRAM OF SOCIAL REFORM

est kind of knowledge, to grasp the ultimate truths.

In Cardinal Newman's "Letters" there is a passage in which he expresses the opinion that to prove a great idea is beyond the capacity of ordinary minds. Great men alone can prove great ideas, he says—or grasp them. He is evidently of the same opinion as "the Master of them that know." But if this view is correct, then the definitely human quality whereof we are in search will be met with in only a small minority of human beings. The really competent thinkers are few, the mental processes of the bulk of mankind, on matters not concerning immediate need, being illogical and haphazard. And thus we shall not escape the inference that only a very few human beings are truly human. The rest will seem nature's adumbrations to the human type. Nature, like an unskilled, unsure craftsman, essayed many a time to fashion a man. She failed in the majority of instances, and the great mass of our fellow-beings are her failures. It was on some such ground as this that Aristotle justified a hierarchical, aristocratic constitution of society, resting on slavery at the bottom. If fellowman means fellow-thinker, and thinker is equivalent to correct and forcible thinker, competent to grasp the highest truths, then it is certain that the multitude does not consist of truly human beings, but of creatures fractionally human, occupying some sort of middle station between the dumb brute and illustrious man.

Should we substitute scientist or artist for thinker, the conclusion will still be the same. Whenever we put the accent of the human upon any of the so-called higher qualities—I care not which—we shall inevitably exclude the majority from the conception of the human. We shall in theology have stripped off Calvinism, or the doctrine of the elect, only to fall back on it in sociology. Nietzsche, or some other scorner of the vulgar herd, if not Aristotle, will become our teacher and guide.

Now to escape this revolting outcome of reflection there is only one way. We must rest the title of every man to be considered fellow-man, not on any quality that has been realized in some few members of the species, but in some quality that exists potentially in all. All or none, must be our watchword, and not in any of the higher qualities may we seek our human title to distinction, but in the very highest; not in the Good, but in the Best. In respect to the

AN ETHICAL PROGRAM OF SOCIAL REFORM

higher, men differ; in respect to the better they differ; in respect to the best they will be found to agree. To base securely the doctrine of our common humanity, it is necessary to discover the common factor which attaches to every member of the human race. That common factor is the potentially best that exists in each.

If it is necessary to propose a definition of this highest and best, I should say that it is the sense of organic connection with others, the consciousness of the individual that in his inmost self he is socially determined, the sense that to live means to live in others without surrender of self; or, more precisely, to exercise such influence on others as to bring to the birth new life conjointly in them and in oneself.[1]

For what does it mean to do good to others, or to serve them? Is it to feed, to clothe, to bring them back to health when sick; to instruct their minds, or minister to their pleasures? All these are instrumental goods. What is the ultimate good or the end to which these are subservient? If we think out the thought of service to its last term, what is the essential, the

[1] The ethical formula which I prefer to use is: So act as to elicit the best in others, and in so doing you will be gradually transformed into the image of what is ideally best in yourself.

incomparable service we are to render others? Is it not to spiritualize them, to make them aware (effectually, so as to give effect in thought and deed to the awareness) that they stand in organic, *that is, spiritual,* relations of give and take with all kindred life whatsoever? And to accomplish this task, even to the slightest extent, will tax the spiritual quality in ourselves to the utmost, summoning it forth by the strain we put upon it, so that jointly with the fellow-beings over whom we lovingly labor we ourselves shall be changed for the better, in the direction of the best. The idea of joint responsibility for the attainment in each of the ultimate aim of life should take the place of egoism and altruism alike.

There is something precious in every human being. That something is buried deep. How deep! We are to bring it to light. This is our major premise. Without it the doctrine of the worthwhileness of every human being would be a glittering falsehood. That there is this hidden preciousness is the primary postulate of ethics. What it is we do not know. We lay it down that it must be there. It is our business to go in quest of it. Everyone has some gift, something he can contribute. But the gift

AN ETHICAL PROGRAM OF SOCIAL REFORM

itself, the talent, as a part of man's natural equipment, is not the spiritual quality in him, that distinctively human thing in him which we seek.[1] It is the gift or talent so used as to awaken the dormant gifts in others that becomes ethically transmuted. It is the reaction of power on power, of life on life, that changes an accident of our nature into an ethical force. *The ethical system is a system of reactions.* The ethical personality is a reagent, one who measures the worthwhileness of what he does and what he is by the effect he produces on others—in the last analysis by the influence he exerts to induce others to subject themselves to the same test.

The idea of so living as to release the life that is in others is capable of appealing to humble people. It is the heart of the matter in all modes of self-sacrifice. Self-sacrifice is indeed an ambiguous term. It is the things of the lesser self that are sacrificed, while the larger self is every time affirmed. This miraculous way of living in others without surrendering self is exemplified in rude and seemingly commonplace

[1] Else the art of the homicide Cellini, the synthetic skill of the chemist, or the knack of the craftsman, would be the basis of our ethical system, and we should be following along the lines of Aristotle.

ways by mothers in the slums who "work their finger-nails off" to keep the children at school so that they may have a better chance; by striking workmen who face starvation rather than submit to what they regard as injustice to their class. The idea of the *dynamic interpotency* of lives supplies the ideal element in the finest types of friendship, in the most nearly perfect marriages. And in proportion as coöperation shall be more widely practiced, and as the social connections shall work themselves out in more and more complex patterns, it will furnish us with new rules of behavior and an enlarged moral code as much superior, perhaps, to that now recognized, as ours is to that of primitive man.

If now we look back on the course we have traversed, we find the following outstanding. First: Beware how you look on a man, how you think of him. As you think of him so you will treat him. If you regard him as a thing, you will spurn him as a thing when occasion arises.

Second, the aim of social reform cannot be, even provisionally, to secure a more equitable distribution of the material goods—that is, to give men an abundance of the things that minister to their physical needs. *Man is a spirit,*

AN ETHICAL PROGRAM OF SOCIAL REFORM

and if you would help him you must touch him at the point of his spiritual being, which is the truth of his being.

Third, the distinctively human attribute is not to be found in the higher qualities, in respect to which there is the greatest diversity, but in the highest quality of all; not in that which has been actualized in anyone, but in that which is potential. The claim that all men are morally equal, the foundation on which democracy is to be built up, is to be founded on the spiritual possibilities that exist in all, however diverse in value their expression.

Again, this doctrine that to live rightly is to live so as to release the life in others, endures the test to which every genuine ethical principle must submit; it is capable of being applied by those who are lowest in the social scale, as well as by the most educated and refined.[1]

There are certain questions which may now be asked us, and which must be met as directly as possible. One of them is often put thus: When you make the liberation of the spiritual nature in men the aim of social reform, are you not in danger of becoming indifferent to the

[1] Denial of the lesser self in order that the higher self may appear and evoke its correlative in another is present in all fine relations. It is the essence of their fineness.

betterment of their material environment? There are the dismal, foul, reeking dwelling-places in the poorer quarters of great cities; there are the children dying by the thousands for lack of proper care and nourishment; there are the overtaxed women; there is the desperate army of the unemployed; there is the relentless exploitation of the weak by the strong, the struggle for existence going on in the bosom of society incessantly. Do not these conditions demand attention first and foremost? Ought we not to postpone concern for the spiritual needs of men until at least these crying physical wants have been satisfied? Is there any use in trying "to save a man's soul on an empty stomach"? It is such arguments as these that one hears constantly, and they have given rise to the kind of materialism that is at present characteristic of social reform. The more thoughtful social workers, of course, as I have said, admit that a man has a certain higher nature—call it by the antiquated name of soul or by any other that you prefer—but they do not admit the necessity of defining the higher nature. It is enough, they think, to take it for granted. Meantime, whatever the man's higher self may be, his body must be fed and clad and

AN ETHICAL PROGRAM OF SOCIAL REFORM

kept from perishing. And this mode of reasoning does often carry conviction with it because it seems based on common-sense and at the same time appeals most intensely to the sympathetic feelings.

But by this passionate plea for the concentration of thought and effort on material improvement the real issues are obscured, which are these: whether human beings can be cut in half —as it were, the bodily part and the higher part isolated from each other, the bodily part being first cared for and then the soul; whether we can afford to leave the notion of the higher nature in the vague; whether in that case the means will not usurp the place of the end; whether we shall not fall into the error of the miser who hoards gold and forgets its uses. Suppose for the moment that we base the work of social reform on sympathy instead of spirituality; suppose that, being sensitive ourselves to pain and pleasure, we make it our chief concern to diminish the pain and increase the pleasures of the poor, shall we not thereby kindle a thirst which there is no possibility of assuaging, the desire for pleasure being unlimited? And will sympathy work as it is expected to? Does not observation show that it is subject to a law of periodicity, culminating and then subsiding? Is it the kind of steady force that is needed to sustain the work of social reconstruction?

Above all, to answer the question we are asked to face: Does the ideal of the spiritual possibilities of man make us less attentive to his physical need? I claim that the exact contrary is true. Better dwellings, assured material existence, are indispensable means to the unfolding of the spiritual possibilities of man. And the more clearly and distinctly we envisage the end, the more intensely shall we desire the end, if it commend itself. And the more intensely we desire it, the more we shall be impelled to adopt the means that conduce to it. How can I be lax or negligent in changing the bad environment if I realize definitely the noble turn in human life to which such a change may lead? He who looks upon man as a higher sort of animal may perhaps be complacently satisfied with even small improvements, as, for example, the little cottage of the workingman with a plot of ground surrounding it, the eight-hour work-day, the children going to school, etc.—in a word, the Philistine's ideal of a happy people, borrowed from the middle class plan of living,

AN ETHICAL PROGRAM OF SOCIAL REFORM

toned down somewhat and extended to the whole population. But he who sees in man a being possessed of infinite worth, *how can he be content with anything short of conditions that will make possible the unfolding of that worth?* How can he find tolerable a state of things as now existing which implies, so far as outward conditions can, the frustration in men of all that is best? If we see a beggar in rags, we may be moved to pity; but if we see a king in rags, are we not stirred to indignation as well as pity; are we then able to bear the disgrace of it? Do we not feel ourselves humiliated by so unseemly a sight? Well, then, if we have learned to look upon every man as in some sense royal, shall we not be all the more constrained to free him and ourselves from the disgrace?[1]

---

[1] The belief that emphasis of the spiritual side of man must lead to the neglect of material improvement is based on the other-worldly conception of spirituality. This led in the past to inadequate endeavors to save people's souls by missionary enterprises, the establishment of Sunday-schools, the erection of chapels, etc., in the slums—the horrible conditions themselves evoking little protest and remaining on the whole untouched. Such a notion of spirituality has nothing in common with our view. The physical, so far from being negligible, is instrumental to the spiritual end. What I contend for is that the motive that leads to physical improvement will be immeasurably strengthened if the high end to be subserved is kept distinct before the mind.

THE WORLD CRISIS AND ITS MEANING

Another searching question is this: Does the evocation of the spiritual personality, when regarded as the supreme rule of life, and therefore as the supreme aim of social reform, issue in a distinctive practical program? Does it furnish a plan of action? Hitherto two alternatives have mainly competed for our suffrage: individualistic capitalism and socialism.[1]

The word socialism has at least a dozen different meanings. Anyone who objects to selfish individualism nowadays is apt to call himself a socialist. But the connotation of socialism where it is most widely accepted is that of collectivistic paternalism, and it is in this sense I use the term. Are we then shut up to these two alternatives, or does the spiritual principle furnish us a third? My answer to this would be, functionalism, as against individualism and socialism. The word is abstract, but no more than the other two, and less ambiguous than the second. What it means can be compressed into the following statement: Those who are engaged in business should have a higher aim than merely to increase the output of material

[1] I do not attempt to discriminate between the various types of individualism, and do not include opportunistic social reform, which edges its way forward by rule of thumb, without any even tentative vision of an ultimate outcome.

AN ETHICAL PROGRAM OF SOCIAL REFORM

goods. At present the man engaged in business and in industry can hardly be said to have a higher aim within the confines of his business. The higher things of life for him lie outside his business. But there must be, for industrial production as well as for every other vocational activity, an *intrinsically higher aim*. That aim should be to perfect its function, hence the name "functionalism." A man is not in business primarily to make money, nor even to set an example of the more equitable distribution of wealth (e. g., by profit-sharing). These things are important, but secondary. The real object in business should be the development of the mind and character of the man who engages in business—of every man who engages in it—not only of the head men but of everyone who takes a part, however humble a part. There are manifold ways of developing mind and character, but the work a man does should be the chief matrix of his personal development. In the work of his hands he should discover and unfold his mental and moral self. Salvation must come by work.

When we look at industrial production in the way it is carried on now, we may say that the great change to be brought about is that that

THE WORLD CRISIS AND ITS MEANING

which is now considered the product shall be regarded as the by-product. The material things are now considered the product, and the man who produces the things is treated as a means to an end. The relation should be exactly the reverse. Material goods are by-products, first in the order of necessity, but second in the order of value. The man himself, as he is modeled and shaped inwardly in the course of his work, is to be regarded as the true product.

Every vocational group within society performs a certain function. No vocational group has ever yet performed its proper function in a satisfactory way. This is true of medicine, law, divinity, art, as well as of agriculture, manufactures, commerce. The perfecting of its function is the spiritual aim which each vocational group should set itself. Industrial activity will be relieved of its base implication when those engaged in it shall consciously set up as the aim for the social group to which they belong the increasing perfection of the particular service they are rendering. This means *through the increase of things to ennoble souls.*[1]

[1] Our grossest appetites, instincts and wants, when treated in human fashion, become the support of what is purest and

AN ETHICAL PROGRAM OF SOCIAL REFORM

The main point remains to be stated. Let us exalt function, but let us be extremely careful to bear in mind the necessary interaction of functions. Society is sometimes called an organism. This is grotesquely untrue. Its members are at war with one another. Society is by no means yet an organism—it is to be made such. The spiritual task of humanity may be expressed in the words "continuous effort at organization." No function can be exercised or improved in a detached and separate way. The incidence of its effects will tell on other functions. The measure of the perfection attained is the degree to which such incidence is stimulating and vitalizing.

I have previously defined the ethical agent as a reagent, the ethical system as a system of reactions. We have now reached the ethical view of the object of social reform. The object of social reform as applied to industry is to create such conditions that the work done by the industrial group shall react in a stimulating

holiest in human experience. Thus, the act of eating, or of satisfying hungry stomachs, becomes the occasion for the frequent reunion of the members of a household, and thus promotes family unity and family affection. The sex instinct becomes the basis of marriage, and mere lust is changed into love. The same thought is applied in the text to material wealth-production.

way and a vitalizing way upon the work done by the correlated social groups.

This is abstract, but clear is the concrete equivalent of it. Agriculture, for example, is applied chemistry, applied biology, applied entomology, etc. It is correlated with these sciences. To perfect the function of practical agriculture (that is, the work done by more than half of the human race) means to handle it in such a way that the practical results achieved shall be the means of testing the sciences implicated, and of provoking the advance of these sciences by constantly presenting new problems on which to whet their theories. The perfection of the function of the agriculturist is seen in the reaction upon the sciences on which it is dependent. This reaction itself, consciously adopted as an aim, will mean the elevation of agriculture to the level of a liberal vocation. The farmer, while tilling the soil, will at the same time be tilling his inner mental field. In striving to contribute to the perfection of the function, he will be mentally perfecting himself.

In like manner the industrial group is correlated with the sciences of physics and chemistry, and in its textile and other branches with the fine arts. The spiritual aim of the indus-

AN ETHICAL PROGRAM OF SOCIAL REFORM

trial group is to react upon the sciences and arts which are its own living principles. In a blind, incidental, utilitarian fashion this relation already exists. The application of electricity to manufacture has produced an immense advance in the theoretical knowledge of electricity. The need of replacing natural by artificial dyes has created an entirely new department of chemical research. In the heyday of the Renaissance, when artisans were artists, and artists artisans, the crafts acquired beauty, the arts significance. The connection is evident enough. But hitherto, in industry at least, the relation has been the polar opposite of what it should be. Pegasus has been harnessed to the yoke. Science, save by the few elect, has been regarded as the calf to be fattened. Or, more exactly, the relation was one-sided. Science was to yield its output of knowledge in order to increase material wealth, but the testing and provocative effect of industrial applications on the progress of science itself was slurred over. By a strange shortsightedness, the higher faculties of man have been summoned to be subservient to the lower, the noble ministry of mind has been enslaved to comfort and convenience. The business of social reform is to elevate every group embraced within society, the industrial group among the rest. To elevate the industrial group means to treat wealth accumulation as a by-product, the effect on the man being the true objective. The man as industrial worker is to be uplifted by thinking of himself as a vitalizing reagent on the science and art involved in his work. The aim of industrial life should be to bring about conditions in which every worker in industry shall be able consciously to participate in the task set to his group as a whole.

It has sometimes been said that the end in life which each man should propose to himself is to leave the world a happier place to live in than he found it. In view of the situation of the world as it exists before us, that were a task of which the feasibility is more than dubious. A better formulation is: *So work that the work of the world shall be better done because you have worked in it.*[1]

---

[1] The ideal cannot be set too high. Whether it be attainable or not is not the primary question. We must strive towards it, and nothing but the highest as an ideal should content us. In the case of agriculture, the fundamental human occupation, this ideal does not seem entirely remote. Every tiller of the soil can to-day be something of a scientist, and can, in modest fashion, take up the advancement of science as his aim. Our agricultural colleges, and especially the agricul-

AN ETHICAL PROGRAM OF SOCIAL REFORM

And now, for those of us who look in the direction that has been indicated, what immediate course of action will be required? How, from our point of view, shall we prosecute the rural high schools that are spreading throughout the country, ought to prepare the way for a race of agriculturists who can, in more or less adequate fashion, carry out this conception. In the case of industry, the problem is vastly more difficult. The relief of industry from the blight of drudgery that rests upon the majority of industrial workers may perhaps be found in the following directions: 1. Combination of agriculture with industry. 2. The pushing of automatism further and further along, so that it may increasingly supplement merely unillumined mechanical operations. 3. The classing of monotonous labor in the same category as excessively onerous labor; that is to say, shortening the hours and multiplying the shifts, so that a man or woman shall be expected to work at mere machine tending only a limited number of hours, and be set free for labor involving freer action of the mind during the remainder of the working hours. 4. The development of new finishing industries, crafts and other occupations in which the personal element is the predominant factor.

The distinction between this view and that of socialism as commonly taught is that the latter seems to despair of redeeming the worker through his work—an aim which, however difficult, we must never let go—and would satisfy the higher needs of human nature by dividing the day into a period of soulless drudgery and a period of study and play. But study and play can by no means afford lasting satisfaction. According to the view outlined above, the day would be divided into a drudgery period, which may be regarded as the toll paid to the exigencies of the human situation, and a period in which the worker will follow some true vocation, one from which he will derive the mental sustenance and enlargement we have described.

197

business of social reform? For one thing, we shall be earnestly enlisted in all the excellent betterment movements now under way: in the movements for Better Housing, for the Minimum Wage, for the Abolishment of Seasonal Employment and of Unemployment, in the fight against tuberculosis and other preventable diseases. Whatever can be done by private enterprise or by collective intervention to secure the improvement of the human instruments in whom the scheme of a spiritualized society is to be worked out will come home to us with an irresistible appeal. How can we be less interested than others in the amelioration of material conditions if we have steadily before our eyes the sublime superstructure of which these conditions are to be the foundation?

But there are certain additional features which more especially will call out our efforts.

We shall pity the mental poverty of the multitude of workers even more than their material indigence. Anyone who is at all sensitive about the "needs of the soul" must find the dulling and deteriorating effect, on the minds of the majority, of their daily occupation even more unbearable than their physical privations. How can the soul on the mental side of it be so

AN ETHICAL PROGRAM OF SOCIAL REFORM

dishonored? Is it really necessary that intellectuality of the more effective kind be confined to the few so-called leaders? Is it a really inevitable concomitant of social evolution that this pall of monotonous labor shall be spread over the masses? Anyone who feels strongly in this way will turn vigorously to the task of bringing mental salvation to the unskilled or half-skilled laborer—for instance, by vastly improving the training of apprentices (using interest in the trade as the starting-point for generous culture), by continued education of the adult worker, by establishing trade museums in and out of factories, by any and every means that will take away the mechanical, routine character of labor. A machine may be defined as a piece of mentality petrified in matter. Mechanical labor is dead labor, the everlasting repetition of the same incorporated idea. Intelligently fruitful labor is of such a kind as constantly to suggest to him who does the work new ways of doing it. We shall try to substitute living labor for dead labor.

We shall fervently help in the movement for better external conditions; we shall spend assiduously our force in crowding mechanical labor more and more on to the machine, where it belongs, and in giving even the laborer farthest down the kind of mental prodding which will make him a reagent on the progress of science.

But we shall be preëminently interested in emancipating the will of the workers. The human quality is to be revealed, not only on its intellectual, but also and especially on its volitional side. It is the obstruction and stultification of the will of the factory operatives, quite as much as the blunting of their minds, that calls for relief. A man is not respected as a man unless a sphere be allotted him for the independent exercise of his will. Independence, rightly understood, and manhood are inseparable ideas. An adult person should not be treated as a child. A child is required to obey orders, to do as he is told—that is, to act from the will of another person rather than from his own. In the case of a child, however, the tutelage is only provisional, the object being to prepare him for the exercise of freedom when he shall come of age. But factory operatives in this respect are treated with less consideration than children. They are expected simply to obey orders, to do as they are told, all day long to carry out rules which they have had no share in making. Moreover, they are supposed

AN ETHICAL PROGRAM OF SOCIAL REFORM

never to come of age so far as their relations to their employers are concerned. They remain under perpetual tutelage in their character as industrial workers. *As the factory operative carries out the idea of another man incorporated in the machine, and not his own idea, so he acts from the will of another man, and not from his own will. And there is no attempt made to train him for freedom!*

Such attempts should be made. We should be moving toward organic democracy in industry. I put emphasis on the adjective "organic." I do not praise what is commonly called industrial democracy. The idea of industrial democracy as commonly proclaimed is copied from the pattern of our political democracy, and it has the same radical defects—defects now so glaringly manifest. It has for its unit the individual, and the conception of society underlying it is that of an aggregate.

But society should be evolved into an organism, and the organic conception should be applied everywhere—to the parts as well as to the whole. The great organism of society should include and consist of minor organisms. The chief industries, for instance, should be minor organic groups, and their free and independent functioning would be their salient, distinctive feature as against the kind of arrangement contemplated by socialism.[1]

The steel industry, for example, would constitute a minor organic group. Its acknowledged object would be the rendering of a certain social service in the best possible way. In the government of the group every worker would participate. His will would be emancipated by giving it effect on the decisions to which he is to be subject. There would be *an industrial parliament* for the trade. The jurisdiction of this parliament, at first limited, would be gradually enlarged. Representation in it would be by branches or departments of the trade. Each worker would vote, not as an isolated unit, but as a member of his department, or branch. The object would be to secure that in the general conduct of the industry due account be taken of the conditions on which depends the human development of the workers in each branch.

I do not advocate turning over our factories immediately to the complete control of the workers. Considering their inexperience, and

[1] This independence does not exclude a certain amount of supervision by the commonwealth as a whole.

AN ETHICAL PROGRAM OF SOCIAL REFORM

in great part their inefficiency, due to lack of education and opportunity, such a step would be extremely premature. But if we see what is wrong, and also what is right, why cannot we work in the direction of the right? The *constitutional government of industry*, as a bridge between the despotic or paternalistic government now in use and organic democracy, should be the next step. Toward that goal ethically-minded persons should advance.

The point of view here stated can be sharply defined by contrasting it with socialism. On the one side we have as the chief aim increase of the product and more equitable distribution of the product; on the other side, as the chief aim, the development of the producer. (It is assumed that the requisite augmentation of the product will inevitably follow and be more securely attained when the higher aim is kept in view.) On the one hand aggregate democracy pushed to its extreme, on the other hand organic democracy in the industrial and, we may add, in the political field as well.[1] On the one

---

[1] According to our conception, political representation, like industrial, should have as its electoral units the organic groups of society instead of individuals. Thus, the farmers, the merchants, the various industrial divisions would be represented as such in the lower houses of our legislatures, and each

THE WORLD CRISIS AND ITS MEANING

hand, justice expressed in terms of material or hedonistic benefits; on the other hand, justice presented as the sum total of the thoughts and acts which tend to facilitate the emancipating reaction of life on life.

We started out by asking what a man who possesses advantages to which on any ground of desert he does not feel himself entitled can do to save his self-respect. The answer was, first, to live the simple, better the essential, life. "A man can be a man even in a palace."

Next, to use his advantages as responsibilities in the sense of promoting the further development of society toward the ethical goal, and the searching question was put: In what direction, then, should he strive? What actually should he try to do? On this issue I have submitted my three propositions: (*a*) To take

---

citizen would vote in the *comitia* of his vocation. This system of representation might be called vocational representation. Women workers would vote in the group with which they are connected as workers. Those who are not engaged in any industry or profession would vote in a separate group of their own. The idea would be that every voter should vote about the things with which he or she is in touch, which he or she understands, and that through the conferences of the representatives of his group with those of other groups as reported back, he shall learn to acquiesce in *that reciprocal adjustment of ends and interests* from which flows the harmony of the State.

AN ETHICAL PROGRAM OF SOCIAL REFORM

part in the material betterment movements. (*b*) To make it his distinctive aim to release the imprisoned mentality of the worker so as to enable him to bear his part in perfecting the social function of his group. (*c*) To work toward organized democracy by introducing constitutionalism in industry as a bridge. The program, whatever its value, is clear-cut, and its relation to the underlying principles is stringent.

When all is said and done it remains the fact that we have advantages, even if we do use them as responsibilities. That we can so use them is itself a privilege to which we are not entitled through any merit of our own. And many of us are troubled by the intrinsic ethical contradiction in our position which is thus left unexpunged. If the work of social change could be pushed rapidly, if essential transformations could be achieved by a spirited attack all along the line on the evil and injustice that exist, the scruple would not be so torturing; the strain upon conscience would be less severe. But social change of a really effective kind is and will be extremely slow, and in the meantime we are on upper levels, and the multitude of our fellow-beings are perishing in the depths.

Perhaps the sting of this reproach cannot be

wholly extracted. At least this is not the place to grapple with the ultimate problem involved. But there is at least one consoling thought that can be offered; *we can contribute on the upper level to solve the problem of those on the lower levels.* Organization of life is the key to the solution. We can set the example of organization. We can organize our relations to the members of our families. We can introduce the principle of organic coöperation into the faculties of schools and colleges, into professional bodies, and groups of religious leaders. The way we look on people is everything. We can look on those with whom we immediately associate organically—that is, spiritually, testing our own human quality ever by the manner in which we react on them. And we can thus prepare the way for the application of the same principle, the same rule of behavior in the lower field, where the dust of material issues as yet obscures the atmosphere and makes faint the nobler vision.

VIII

ETHICAL DEVELOPMENT EXTENDING THROUGHOUT LIFE

THE principal thought to be embodied in the following outline is that the life of a human being from the point of view of its ethical aim, should be regarded as a series of ascending terraces, each succeeding one rising above its predecessors.

This view of ethical development—it may be called the vertical view—is in sharp contrast to the prevailing horizontal view. According to the latter, the ethical demands are practically identical in all periods of life, whatever the circumstances in which the individual may be placed. According to the former, each period of life has its distinctively dominant ethical note. In each period some one duty or set of duties rises paramount, some one ethical aspect shines out, some special ethical lesson is to be learned. The ultimate goal, indeed, remains the same: it is the summit of the mountain towards which the successive terraces rise. It is ever in view, it is always the aim. The chief ethical rule also remains unchanged. But the successive applications of it to new relations are not mere illustrations: rather are they revelations of the deeper meaning of the rule and they lead to a more penetrating insight into the nature of the ethical aim itself.

The importance of these considerations as marking a new attitude towards the problem of moral education is evident. Those who adhere to the horizontal view will think of moral education chiefly as concerned with the teaching and training of the young. "Moral education" means for them the imparting of a certain body of moral doctrine and the fixing of appropriate habits. And the task of the moral educator will seem to be approximately finished when he has furnished the rising generation, once and for all, with the lamp which is to enable them to see their way. It is true, no one will deny that moral self-education must be continued throughout the whole of life. But for those who take the attitude indicated, moral progress through self-education simply means increased power to hold fast the principles inculcated in one's youth, greater promptness in responding to the

ETHICAL DEVELOPMENT THROUGH LIFE

call of duty and a more delicate tact in applying the recognized principles to the unraveling of tangled moral problems. It does not mean gaining new light on the meaning and content of the ethical aim itself.

If, on the contrary, one takes the "terrace" view of ethical development, the problem of the moral education of the young assumes an entirely new and different aspect. The moral education of the young will then be the first introductory stage of a long development, and it is clear that the first stage cannot be wisely or adequately planned without distinct reference to what is to follow. The attempt, at least, will have to be made to map out the entire course and system of ethical development with a view of fitting the first beginnings into this system. For each stage is to yield certain gains that are to be taken up and to be further ripened in the succeeding stage. And it is plain that without a more or less explicit conception of the series as a whole, the work done on any one term of the series will fail of its best results. "Without the truth," says Thomas à Kempis, "there is no knowing; without the way, there is no going." The truth in this case is the knowledge of the contribution which each period of life may be expected to yield toward the development of human personality. Without this truth, there is no real knowing in respect to the task of the moral educator, be he concerned with the education of the young or with the problems of adult self-education. And without the way there is no going, and the truth must point the way.

The lack of any distinctly conscious perception of the moral problems that stand out in the different periods and relations of life is one of the chief causes, not only of moral failure and shipwreck in individual instances, but of the generally low moral estate of men at the present day when compared with their notable achievements in the intellectual field. In any case the movement for moral education, so long as its point of view is mainly restricted, as at present, to children of the school age, will remain shorn of its brightest promise and of the sublimity of suggestion which rightly belongs to it.

Prior to sketching in rough outline a course of ethical development extending throughout life, let me present briefly the point of view from which the whole course is conceived.

The ethical aim is the development of per-

ETHICAL DEVELOPMENT THROUGH LIFE

sonality. Personality is to be distinguished from individuality. The individual, insofar as ethicized, is a personality. Empirical man, with his defects and his qualities, is an individual—one of a kind. Empirical man, insofar as he is transformed in subjection to the rational ideal, is a personality.

This difference involves also a fundamental difference between value and worth. An individual has value, a personality has worth. Value applied to human beings is the property which one man has of satisfying the needs or wants of another. Worth is the intrinsic preciousness or worthwhileness which belongs to a man on his own account. The concept of worth is altogether an ideal concept. To ascribe worth to men is to ascribe to them an ideal character in no wise justified by their actual behavior. It is to invest them with a glory which their performances nowise warrant. It is to see them in a manner *sub specie aeternitatis;* that is to say, as indispensable components of a rational universe. The concept of worth is founded on a postulate, rather than on a fact; it is based on the assumption that there exists in every man potentially some unique distinctive excellence, some mode of necessary being induplicable outside himself. Let us adopt for a moment the sublime fiction of the harmony of the spheres, only replacing the shining stars by mental and moral beings, stars in a spiritual universe. Let us assume that there is an infinite number of such beings. Let us assume that each of these beings is capable of sounding forth a divine note expressive of his inmost nature, without which the worldwide harmony would be incomplete. Let us assume further that each of these musical utterances has the quality of eliciting in utmost purity their genuine note from each of the infinite members of this innumerable multitude of beings: we shall then have a kind of pictorial statement of the thought here presented. We shall also be helped to apprehend imaginatively the meaning of the formula which is now to be offered as the chief ethical principle or rule, controlling and determining the course of ethical development in all the successive periods. *So act as to release the best in others, and thereby you will release the best that is in yourself.* Or, *So act as to assist in bringing to light the unique excellence in others, and thereby you will bring to light the unique excellence that is in yourself.* Or, more pre-

ETHICAL DEVELOPMENT THROUGH LIFE

cisely still, *So act as to evoke in another the efficient idea of himself as a member of the infinite organism, and thereby corroborate in yourself the same efficient idea with respect to yourself.* For it must be remembered that the latent distinctive excellence which is here taken as the foundation of worth or personality is not a static, but a dynamic quality. It is not to be discovered by isolating man, by seeing him detached from his fellows. The idea of worth is a social idea. It deals with man in his relations. It sees in him a being essentially active, whose very life consists in affecting the life of others. Worth, therefore, may be defined as that which provokes worth in others, distinctive excellence as that which calls forth a reaction in others in the direction of their distinctive excellence. Ethics becomes a science of reactions.[1]

---

[1] For a fuller account of the positions condensed in the above, the reader is referred to the author's article in the *International Journal of Ethics,* October, 1911. It may be asked, with what right the private ethical philosophy of the writer is thus submitted for the use of those who may not at all agree with his point of view. The answer is that ethical philosophies or theories are to be judged by their fruit; that is, by the practical directions to which they lead. If these be sound, or even suggestive, they may be accepted to that extent by those who would wholly reject the premises from which they are derived. In this way much of the ethical prog-

THE WORLD CRISIS AND ITS MEANING

Regarding, then, the pilgrimage of the human spirit through time as a kind of *progressus ad Parnassum*, with an ever-expanding outlook on the ethical field and with the finest ethical results to come at the end; regarding the ethical aim of life as that of finding oneself through right penetration into the life of others, and setting before ourselves that the ethical task consists in taking empirical human nature as it exists and transforming it, we shall not fail to perceive that in each of the successive periods the empirical facts are such as necessarily to give rise to specific ethical tasks. The ethical task cannot be the same for the immature child and the full-grown man in the complete exercise of his mental faculties. It cannot be quite the same for the single and the married. It cannot be the same for those who follow different callings, each calling having its own moral perils, its own moral opportunities. It cannot be quite the same for one who is charged with the full responsibilities of active life and for one who is permitted to spend the remainder of his days

---

ress which mankind has actually achieved has been brought about. We adopt certain of the fruits of Stoicism without endorsing the Stoic pantheism. We accept many of the Christian precepts without necessarily subscribing to the formulated Christian creed.

as a spectator. It is of capital importance that these problems, these perils and opportunities, shall be analyzed and presented in definite terms. Here, as has been said, only a few hints will be attempted.

CHILDHOOD

The salient fact about a child is its dependence on adults. The ethical task in this period is to profit by the dependence in order to lay the foundations of future independence. The question at the outset is (and it will constantly recur later on): How can the circumstances in which a human being is placed, the accidents of this temporal development and estate, be utilized so as to promote the unique distinctive excellence, which is the goal?

As far as the first period is concerned, the means to be employed seem to be chiefly the following: Bring home to the child the fact that there is such a thing as a kingdom of worth, a society in which moral striving counts as the highest form of human activity. This can be done, and can be done only by the worth which shines out from the faces, the speech and conduct of the adults with whom the child is brought into contact. Spiritual ideas at this stage are far beyond the comprehension of the young, but spiritual impressions, to be retained and understood later on, are capable of being received. The afflatus of a moral world should radiate upon the child's life from the persons of its elders. The key to moral education of the young, as the preponderant majority of writers on the subject agree, is the moral attitude of those who undertake to educate the young. And by the moral attitude we are to understand principally the unremitting effort in the direction of the moral ideal and the reverence that finds its expression in such effort. Reverence toward older persons, especially toward parents and teachers, is the specific virtue of childhood. Reverence is aroused only toward those who themselves revere.[1]

In the next place, the sense of the organic, inseparable relation with other fellow-beings is to be fostered by parental love, by a kind of love that is unbought, unmerited as yet, but not

---

[1] Here we have an exemplification of the chief moral rule, *Seek to release the best in others and thereby you will release it in yourself*. Reverence toward parents is the key virtue in the moral system of childhood. In order to awaken this feeling in the child, the parent must revere something higher than himself and he must be continually growing in reverence, in order to give to his child the essential moral preparation.

ETHICAL DEVELOPMENT THROUGH LIFE

therefore unconditioned, a love that may on occasion manifest itself by inflicting punishment and pain, and yet is felt to be the disinterested love, none the less.

Next, the incipient personality of the child is to be honored by the strict observance of impartiality and fairness in dealing with the child. The actual assertion of personality really involves freedom from the constraint exercised by others. Such freedom, except in extremely limited measure, is not yet possible for a young child. Children are dependent and must learn to act under rules laid down by their superiors. Being thus in a state of dependence, the consciousness of personality and of that moral equality which is the mark of personality manifests itself in the demand on their part that they shall be treated as *equal dependents;* that the rules which they are compelled to obey shall be applied equally to all alike. There is no one thing that children so much resent as unfairness, or undue discrimination in favor of one of their number, whether by parents or teachers. There is no subject which school children discuss so frequently among themselves as the real or supposed partiality of one of their teachers, no subject on which they refine to such lengths of casuistry. And this should put us on our guard with respect to the incalculable injury that may be done by deviations from the strict lines of justice in matters that may seem to us trivial. It is important not only that we be just in our treatment of children, but, as far as possible, that we also seem to be just.

With the help of reverence, love, and equitable rules, the children are to acquire those indispensable habits which form the substructure of the whole moral edifice of their future lives: the habits of self-control, of order, of gentleness and consideration, the habits of industry and application, etc. But without the sentiment of reverence, without the filial love that responds to the parental love, without the primary respect for equity and law, these habits alone will prove but a feeble and treacherous foundation to build upon.

It may be added that the child is also to obtain its first initiation into the ideas of the state and of religion chiefly by means of the reverberations which these ideas awaken in the life of its elders. The piety of parents and teachers, their loyal citizenship, will reflect itself on the feelings of the young.

ETHICAL DEVELOPMENT THROUGH LIFE

ADOLESCENCE

The salient fact about the child is dependence. The outstanding fact about the adolescent is the craving for independence coupled with the necessity for continued dependence because of inexperience and immaturity. The ethical task is to use this craving as a means of advancing a step toward actual independence.

At about the age of puberty, a critical change occurs. The consciousness of separateness is accentuated. The human atom gets loose, as it were, from the molecule. The individual escapes or seeks to escape from the social context and its constraint.

The ethical task at this time is to assist the adolescent in reconstructing his world, in reintegrating himself into the social whole on the basis of consent rather than of compulsion. And here there are three kinds of relation that demand particular attention: the compulsory relations, the pure choice relations, and the choices which eventually lead to compulsory relations. Of the first kind, the most important are the filial or family relations. From the bonds of filial and fraternal duty no one can ever escape. To reconstruct, so far as these are concerned, can only mean to revise, to understand more finely, to voluntarily assume that which hitherto was more or less imposed from without. The best turn that can take place in the relation of adolescents toward parents is based on this new voluntariness of attitude. The adolescent is to become consciously the companion of the parent. The child ignorantly idealizes father and mother, ascribing to them every kind of perfection and regarding them as a kind of earthly providence, as beings who have no needs of their own, but exist to satisfy those of others. The point of view of the adolescent is to undergo a change in both particulars. The reverence he feels for them is to attach, not to the unreal perfections with which he clothes them, but to the earnest striving after the nobler things of life which he discerns in them. And instead of regarding them as godlike givers, free from want and limitation, his eyes are to be opened so as to see the actual needs and the limitations, physical, mental, or social, under which they carry on the struggle of life. To assist them, if only by understanding sympathy, should be his highest aim.

Of the second class, the pure choice relations, friendship is the most important. The adoles-

ETHICAL DEVELOPMENT THROUGH LIFE

cent should be helped to the right conception of the specific office of friendship in the development of personality. A comparative study of the ideals of friendship, as held by the Pythagoreans, Aristotle, Kant, Emerson, etc., will be found useful.

Of the choices which eventually lead to compulsory relations, the choice of a calling is perhaps the best example. It is true, one can select a certain vocation and, finding oneself mistaken, later on exchange it for another. Yet the rule should be: initial carefulness in the choice, with the presumption of permanent persistence in it later on. A broad outlook on the system of human callings should be opened up at this time, the nature of the different callings, the faculties they bring into play, the aptitudes they require, should be described; above all, the ideal aim of vocational life should be set forth.

Of the dangers which beset the path of the adolescent, the principal one is prematureness, in all its forms—premature assertion of independence, leading to defiance of authority and foolish contempt for advice; prematureness in the sex relation; prematureness in the attempt to obtain a fugitive notoriety (as in athletic contests) by achievements lying within the reach of the mentally immature. Undue concentration of effort on such parerga of human development tends to sterilize the mind and to prevent success later on in the real business of life. The moral educator may rest fairly satisfied with his results if he is able to influence the young so that they shall be willing to spend endless toil on preparation and renounce fruition for the present. The virtue of the adolescent is postponement. The reward of the adolescent is the noble forecast, the golden vision, of what he may be able to accomplish when his powers shall be ripened.

Of the topics of ethical instruction in this period, the first and foremost is the idea of worth. This is the cornerstone of the entire ethical edifice. The points to bring out are that independence, or the right of self-determination, is based on the worth which is inherent in human nature, and that the worth of any one human being is conditioned on the recognition of worth in all others.[1]

[1] The study of the history of human slavery, the history of the Peasants' War in Germany and of the long-drawn-out struggle of the laboring class for better conditions, is useful as a means of arousing indignation at the mistreatment of human beings and serves by reaction to strengthen the hold on the student's mind of the idea of the indefeasible dignity and worth of man.

ETHICAL DEVELOPMENT THROUGH LIFE

Other topics are:

The re-interpretation of the duties of the family;

Friendship;

The sex-relation;

The ethics of the vocations; and

A general preliminary account of the ethics of citizenship.[1]

EARLY MIDDLE LIFE

Leading Thoughts:

The work that a man does in his calling is the anvil on which he is to beat out his personality.

The work that a man does is valuable, not chiefly for its results, but for its reaction on the development of the worker. (See what Wilhelm von Humboldt has to say on the bloom as compared to the fruit.)

Every calling is charged with the performance of a certain specific kind of social function or service. No one of the various functions committed to the various callings has ever

---

[1] In this connection, special emphasis should be laid on the ethical side of the state and on the inspiring moments in the history of the nation, rather than on the technical details of the mechanics of government.

yet been adequately performed—not that of the physician, of the priest, of the artist, of the artisan; not the highest any more than the humblest. The aim of anyone who enters a calling should be to carry forward the service or function committed to it to greater perfection. In order to do this, he must deploy his special gift or aptitude. In attempting to do so, he gets possession approximately of his special gift or aptitude. In pursuing an objective task, he realizes a subjective end.

The work is rightly done when done in such a way that the worker grows mentally and morally in the process of doing it.

Mental development is promoted when the work suggests new ways of doing it, while it is being done, and when each problem solved raises up new problems to be solved.

The work, if rightly done, must react on the moral as well as the mental development of the worker.

The two go together. It is useless, except provisionally and for convenience of discussion, to treat them separately.[1]

[1] Moral and intellectual defects seem to have the same root; the same faults which disfigure or narrow a man in point of character will be found to narrow or deflect his thinking.

ETHICAL DEVELOPMENT THROUGH LIFE

The total development of the worker is furthered by the trinity of his relations to superiors, equals, and inferiors; to master-minds, co-workers, and apprentices. It is in these threefold relations that the character of a human being is built up.

Who is a master? The master in one's vocation is the pathfinder, the epoch-making thinker and doer. He who in the strength and illumination of a fresh initiative for a moment catches a glimpse of the entire field and measures—though it be from but one point of view—its dimensions, sees or senses the whole context of its problems. The advantage of mental contact with a master is that of being lifted up with him to something of the same elevation and extent of outlook. One thus acquires a profounder insight into the nature of the problems, though the particular solutions be rejected. One gets the inspiration of the method with which the problems in these illustrious instances have been attacked.

The ancient rule holds true—"Get thee a master."

The relation to the master is the key to the other two. The co-worker or equal is one who is our master in certain respects, we being his followers; and to whom we are masters in other respects, he being our follower.

The relation to the apprentice is to the master that is one day to be.

The great danger that appears in early middle life, that to which the human spirit, striving to attain personality, at this time is particularly exposed, is the false estimate put by others upon our work, and through our work upon ourselves. We cannot, indeed, prevent the formation of false estimates in others' minds, but we can avoid falling into the trap of simply accepting them. The difficulty, indeed, of here steering the middle course is great. On the one side we must respect and bow to the judgment of our fellows and submit to the sharp edge of their criticism; on the other side we must be innovators, and therefore be sure enough of ourselves to defy the judgment even of the majority of our contemporaries. The trinity of relations above described, and especially that to the master-minds, is in this respect our surest safeguard.

LATER MIDDLE LIFE

At this stage of development, the interrelation of one's calling to other callings is the preëminent feature. All the different vocations react upon one another. The progress of the fine arts reacts upon that of the handicrafts, and conversely. The physical sciences are closely interconnected. Science as a whole exercises intimate influence upon philosophy and religion. There is a web of cross-relations.

The chief ethical rule applies: *So exercise your calling as to quicken the vocational activity of all related callings.* Keep well within your boundaries. Do not impertinently intrude into your neighbor's precincts. Be not a vocational jingo. If you are a scientist, for instance, do not assume the right to extend the method of the physical sciences, in imperialistic fashion, over the whole field. But all the same, let the touchstone of success within your own lines be this: that the truth you have apprehended is found acceptable by those who work in different lines; that your life becomes life to them, stimulating them to results differentiated from yours.

THE WORLD CRISIS AND ITS MEANING

The dangers that appear at this time are those of dilettantism at one extreme, and crusty, Philistine specialism at the other.[1]

OLD AGE

The ethical keynote of this period is right abdication. The ethical task is that of making up the balance-sheet of one's past, reviewing the whole course we have run, and unflinchingly setting down its failures as well as its partial successes. There are very few men who would not plan their life differently than they have actually conducted it, if they had the opportunity. Mistakes perhaps were made by others in our early training. Other aberrations there have been for which we have no one to blame but ourselves, due to errors of judgment or moral remissness. We have followed *ignes fatui*. We have mistaken our admirations for our capabilities. We have fought, for years perhaps, under false flags, or with watchwords

---

[1] The problem, how to be delivered from the disastrous effects of specialism, how to know something well without forfeiting the outlook on the whole, is in some sense the most urgent problem of our times. Simplification, and the conscious interrelating of the central principles of one's work to the central principles of others' work, seem to point the way out.

ETHICAL DEVELOPMENT THROUGH LIFE

on our lips, of party or creed, which never really expressed our inmost tendencies.

The ethics of old age is the ethics of abdication. Abdication implies, besides vacating our place, making the way easier for our successor. It has been said that no one can really transmit the benefits of his experience to another; that every new generation must learn the painful lessons afresh. But we can at least facilitate the process of learning these lessons, especially by improving the methods of education and training that obtain in our calling. And we can in addition school ourselves to take the right spiritual attitude toward our successor, whoever he may be, the attitude of welcome towards one of whom we hope that he will eclipse us. *Morituri te salutamus!*

I can but mention here the help to be expected in developing such a scheme from the various empirical sciences—the science which Mill called *ethology*, the psychology of character, the social sciences, etc., all of which must be looked to to fill in the outline.

But it should be noted specifically in what way the social institutions, the family, the state, and the church, can contribute toward the growth of personality. The family, the state, and the church run in a parallel series alongside of the line of development that has been traced. In the family, we are included from the beginning: first in that to which we belong as sons and daughters; afterwards in that to which we belong as fathers and mothers. The family is the organ of the spiritual as well as of the physical reproduction of the human race. The contribution of the family to personality consists in the obligation we are under, as parents, to focalize the results of our development, in order thereby to enkindle spiritual life in our offspring.

The functions of mother and father in this respect are diverse. The man seems to represent the factor of differentiation, the woman that of integration. The process of accommodation that goes on between them quickens the seed of worth in the young.

The state, likewise, envelops us from the beginning and we lay our dust in our country's soil. The state, ethically considered, is the organization of the vocational groups, designed, by the interplay between them, to give expression to the aptitudes or gifts of a people, with a view to building up the particular type of civilization which that people is fitted to

ETHICAL DEVELOPMENT THROUGH LIFE

produce. The moral profit which the individual derives from citizenship is the instruction he receives in the true nature of what is called "the public welfare" (to be defined as the sum of the conditions favorable to the creative activity just described), and the acceptance of this public aim into his private will.[1]

The church, also, is one of the indispensable social institutions. If at the present day it no longer includes the whole of our life, that is so because, in many cases, as an instrument it has broken in the hands of those who desire to use it. The church, ethically speaking, is the vessel of the Holy Grail, in which are forever to be generated the ultimate ideals of mankind, those cosmic ideals which have their source in the social ideals and in turn corroborate them.

In closing this enumeration of crucial

---

[1] Early married life corresponds to the first half of the vocational period, in which the worker acquires a certain degree of superiority and becomes master of the technique of his calling up to date. The second half of married life corresponds to the later vocational period, in which the interrelations are the conspicuous features. At this period the parent has to deal with the problem of directing his growing sons or daughters into their appropriate vocational lines. In the state, as ideally conceived, there should also be *degrees* of citizenship, corresponding to the ripeness achieved.

thoughts about the sciences of life let me add a few words of the last stage of all.

ON THE BRINK

The end is in sight. We have finished our pilgrimage. Have we, then, reached our goal? Have we achieved personality? We are as far from having done so as ever. We measure as we have never done before the distance that separates the finite from the infinite. The paradox that we forever seek to attain that which under earthly conditions is unattainable, remains. The unique, distinctive excellence, latent, but unapparent in us, is unapparent still. It is a star that shines above us in the highest heavens and we are like beings sunk far, far down in the depths of an abyss, looking *de profundis* toward that star. But it is our star, our essential self, the rays that descend to us are compelling; we are subject to it and therefore akin to it.

Thus, we have not, indeed, realized our ideal, but we have realized the reality of our ideal. It subsists in the world of true being, and we with it. And this, I take it, is the final outcome of it all, this the conviction that brightens our eyes as we stand on the brink.

ETHICAL DEVELOPMENT THROUGH LIFE

TO RECAPITULATE

The stages of growth are:

In childhood, right subjection;

In adolescence, reinterpretation of relations and preparation;

In early middle life, reaction of the work so as to elicit the distinctive gift of the worker;

In later middle life, quickening reaction upon interrelated callings—that which at present is treated as incidental to be erected into the chief conscious end;

In old age, right summation of life's results and welcome to successor;

On the brink, the right farewell.

The simile under which life is represented as a hill with an upward incline and thereafter a downward slope may be true of man physically and even intellectually. But it is not true of him spiritually. It need not be. The highest point may be reached at the very end.